Ida Tarbell, Muckraker

Ida Tarbell, Muckraker

by

Frances G. Conn

THOMAS NELSON INC.
Nashville / New York

First edition

Library of Congress Catalog Card Number: 78–181678
International Standard Book Number: 0–8407–6220–8

MANUFACTURED IN THE UNITED STATES OF AMERICA

For Bob, Gob, and Goppa

Contents

7

Ida Tarbell, Muckraker

Foreword

Early in the 1900's a group of talented journalists banded together to fight injustice and the social evils that existed in American society. There was no historical precedent for such an alliance. Nicknamed "muckrakers" by President Theodore Roosevelt, they wrote of high-handed monopolies, food adulteration, misuse of natural resources, unscrupulous business and political practices, child-labor abuses, and the inhuman living conditions of the poor.

The muckrakers dug deep into American life and spoke out with a newfound bluntness. Nothing escaped their scrutiny. They delved into the personal backgrounds of those accused of malpractices. They made private information public.

For the first time in American history the public read the unsavory details of the nation's worst problems and demanded change. Even today, seven decades later, historians agree that the muckraker tradition greatly influenced our present politics, economics, and social thought.

The first muckraker * was a woman—Ida Minerva Tar-

* Some historians credit Lincoln Steffens with being the first muckraker because his article on political corruption was published one month earlier than Ida Tarbell's. Ray Stannard Baker and Mark Sullivan both claimed the title for themselves. Miss Tarbell, however, had been researching her subject several years before the others began.

bell. In 1897 she was assigned by the publisher of a prominent magazine to look into the practices of the Standard Oil Company and report on her findings. Her first article on this subject, which appeared in *McClure's Magazine* in November of 1902, was disarmingly bland. She traced the history of the oil industry and only at the end hinted at what was to come in the next issue. The article in the December issue rocked the nation. It was a shocking exposé filled with sensational revelations. The public, eager for such information, scrambled to buy the magazine. Editors, noting this reaction, encouraged other writers to model their work after Ida Tarbell's.

She wrote seventeen additional articles on the Standard Oil Company, each fanning the nation's growing hostility toward the power and practices of monopolistic corporations and strengthening the movement to outlaw them. In 1911 the Supreme Court of the United States broke up this greatest monopoly of them all.

Despite the emotional impact of her writing and her ability to affect national opinion, Ida Tarbell was neither a powerful nor a rousing personality. She preferred to write on noncontroversial topics, particularly history and biography. She was sensitive, almost shy, and, in the tradition of her journalistic calling, fiercely objective. In her quiet way she left a mark on American history.

I never met Ida Tarbell, but I know her well through the magic of shared experience. We are both products of the northwestern Pennsylvania oil country—three generations apart. Our families, drawn to seek their fortunes in the aftermath of the world's first oil rush, settled in Titusville, Pennsylvania, where Colonel Edwin Drake drilled his famous well.

Ida Tarbell lived there during the area's heyday and

witnessed the dogged struggles of a new industry against the scheming and finagling that followed the oil boom. Seventy-five years later I grew up in the tranquillity of an established oil refining town fifteen miles south of Titusville.

Ida Tarbell attended Allegheny College. So did I. She lived and worked in New York City. So did I. She moved to Washington, D.C. So did I. I have even walked the Parisian streets she loved so well, streets which still teem with students—Saint Germain and le Boulevard Saint Michel.

More than fifty years ago my aunt, then a student at Titusville High School, typed Ida Tarbell's manuscripts, and one of my cousins remembers riding beside "the famous gray-haired lady" in her sleek new electric car.

I have thumbed her papers, read her letters, and listened to old-timers describe her like a legend—"a social reformer," "the noted biographer," "the dean of women authors," "a feminist," and "a stateswoman." Ida Tarbell called herself "a historian." I prefer "the muckraker."

The quoted passages in this book are not imaginary. They are Ida Tarbell's own words, taken from records of actual conversations or from her own writings.

Quotations from letters and documents are authentic, based on materials in Miss Tarbell's original files.

I acknowledge great indebtedness to the Reis Library at Allegheny College in Meadville, Pennsylvania, and to the late Philip M. Benjamin, librarian; to the Drake Well Memorial Library at Titusville, Pennsylvania, and to Mrs. Jane Elder, librarian; and to the Montgomery County, Maryland, library system, particularly Miss Rhodeia Keyser of Davis Library.

1

Pennsylvania or Iowa?

The time was the beginning of November 1857, and a winter chill gripped the tiny farm community of Wattsburg, Pennsylvania. The country was beset by one of its periodic money crises. What had begun as the Panic of 1857 had deepened into a depression. Winter could only make things worse for those who had no money to pay their debts.

All across the troubled nation, mortgages on homes and farms were being foreclosed. No one had money to buy imported luxuries like coffee, chocolate, or sugar. And despite the cold, no one was even thinking about buying a new winter coat.

Unfair as it was, those who had saved money when times were good, making regular deposits at the bank, now suffered most. Banks carried no insurance for the cash entrusted to them, and depositors found their life savings tied up in a failing banking business that was suffering just like every other business in the nation. Banks were closing down everywhere as customers hammered at the locked doors, demanding their money.

Esther Tarbell, a local schoolteacher, had gone like so

many others to the county bank to withdraw her savings. It was travel money—enough to enable her to join her husband out on the Iowa frontier as soon as their child was born. That, she could feel, would be very soon. She walked heavily and slowly until she reached the bank, only to find the door bolted and the window blinds tightly shut. There she stood, her money gone, and her husband more than a thousand miles away, waiting for her.

Of course, things could have been worse. Although the young woman missed her husband, she was comfortable and cared for in her father's story-and-a-half log house. On the well-stocked farm, where physical effort counted more than money, there was always plenty to eat—milk from their own cows, fresh eggs, chicken for Sunday dinner. Just as important, when the time came for the birth of her first baby, Esther would be attended by her mother and neighbor women experienced in childbirth.

On November 5, 1857, Ida Minerva Tarbell was born in her grandfather's log house, but a year and a half was to go by before she saw her father.

Franklin Sumner Tarbell had gone west the previous spring, following the route of other young pioneers. There he hoped to claim some of the rich farmland that lay on the country's frontier and, because he had no money, to build a house with his own hands. He had worked his way through a teacher's academy, managed a fleet of river barges, and worked as a carpenter, but his greatest aspiration was to have his own farm and work his own land.

Off he went through Ohio, Indiana, and Illinois. In his father's youth, this had been the northwest frontier—a country of forests broken only by Indian villages, stockaded towns, and isolated farming settlements. Now it was so well settled that newcomers from the east were pushing across the Mississippi into Iowa, Kansas, and Nebraska. Frank Tarbell, joining their number, had to walk the last 150 miles, but he finally found what he wanted—fertile Iowa land, at the edge of the prairie. Each day an endless stream of covered wagons passed by, carrying families bound for a new life in Nebraska or even farther west.

Franklin, however, was different from most of the settlers who packed family and possessions into a crowded wagon for the bumpy trip west. He preferred that *his* wife, though still in the early months of pregnancy, not endure such rigors. Instead he planned to build a house and have it ready for her arrival. Meanwhile he himself could make do with a bed and a washstand in the settlement's only rooming house.

Without wasting a day's time, he went to a nearby sawmill and applied for a job. He didn't want money, he told the owner. Instead, he wanted to take his pay in lumber. The owner, happy to find a combination employee-customer, readily agreed to hire him. Late each afternoon, after finishing work at the sawmill, Franklin hauled a few more boards out to the site and worked until the night darkness forced him to quit. Then back he went to the rooming house, where in all probability he would sit down to a tasteless portion of cold stewed chicken and potatoes. By the time the house was completed, the Tarbells' savings were meaningless entries in a useless bankbook. Frank and Esther, who had waited through a six-year engagement in order to save money for their marriage, were once again penniless and once again waiting for better times. But the depression only grew worse as the winter gave way to spring. In many places money as a means of exchange had practically disappeared, and people bartered for the goods and services they needed.

Late in the summer of 1858, while President Buchanan struggled to bring back prosperity, Franklin Tarbell decided to wait no longer. He left his farm behind and started back to the east—walking. Two hundred miles on his way he found a school that needed a teacher. There he remained until the following spring, teaching in exchange for his room, board, and the cost of a train ticket back to Pennsylvania.

With the first green leaves of 1859, he returned to Wattsburg, tired and disappointed, a stranger to one-and-a-half-year-old Ida. The little girl resented sharing her mother's affection. "Bad man," she screamed, hiding behind her mother's full skirts whenever he approached. In time, however, she came to accept and to love the big man who had so suddenly come into their lives. But her parents had a harder time solving their money problems.

Once again, Frank left his family, hoping to find work that would pay him enough money to move Esther and Ida to the Iowa farmhouse. There was no work in Wattsburg, but there might be something in Jamestown, New York, where Frank had managed the flat-bottomed river-barge fleet. In spite of the developing railroads, river traffic was still the cheapest and easiest way of transporting people and goods. The barges that left Jamestown followed the Allegheny River southwest to Pittsburgh, Pennsylvania. There they picked up the Ohio River, the great artery of commerce that flowed directly into the Mississippi, carrying settlers westward and bringing eastern products to markets in the South and Midwest.

River life, Frank found, had changed very little in the intervening years. He noticed an increase in the number of steamboats that traveled in and out of Pittsburgh, but there were fewer barges now than in former days. If the

stories being circulated were accurate, many barge workers had quit their jobs and headed for northwestern
Pennsylvania, where a man named Drake had found a way
to drill for crude oil. According to reports, huge quantities
of oil were being pumped out of the ground, and people
were becoming wealthy overnight.

To Frank, the stories didn't make sense. What would
people do with all that oil? As a boy, he had packed
crude-oil grease into the wheels of his father's farm wagons to keep them turning smoothly, and later, while working on the barges, he had burned oil-soaked rags for night
light. The smoky stench still lingered in his memory. He
remembered, too, the crude-oil medicine that his mother
had forced down his throat every time he had a fever or
cold—but certainly the gallons of oil being pumped out
of the ground already exceeded the needs of the wagon
wheels, barge lights, and medicine!

His curiosity whetted, the young man went to Titusville,
Pennsylvania, for a firsthand look at the oil wells springing
up along Oil Creek. The stories were true! The valley was
alive with activity. A ramshackle community, hastily hammered together, lined the banks of Oil Creek.

For the first time Frank saw the oil derricks that he had
heard described. They were four-sided ladderlike struc-
tures reaching thirty feet into the air. From the top of
each hung a thick rope connected at the bottom to a six-
foot iron chisel. Alternately, the chisel rose and fell, its
sharp end plunging deeper and deeper into the earth.

Wherever Frank looked, men were working feverishly
at finding oil. It seemed that a Yale University professor
by the name of Benjamin Silliman had done a chemical
analysis of crude oil and discovered that by boiling the
thick liquid at higher and higher temperatures, he could

distill a variety of products ranging from water, which he discarded, to a group of oils that became thicker and darker with each temperature rise. The most important of these products was a lamp oil that burned clean and gave a clear light. Not only was it safe to burn, but it was cheaper than either coal oil or whale oil. Already the new oil, called kerosine, was driving the other products from the marketplace.

Oil poured out of the wells faster than the drillers could find storage containers. In desperation, men quickly hammered together makeshift wooden tanks that leaked more oil than they held in.

Noting the problem, Frank Tarbell, skilled as a wood joiner, believed he could build a tank with a capacity of five hundred barrels or more. He offered his services to a driller who stood watching a fortune in oil leak away on the ground.

"Show me a model that won't leak, and I'll give you an order," said the man.

With that challenge, Frank was in business.

2

Home in the Oil Region

By the summer of 1860, the Tarbell Tank Shop was well known throughout the oil region. Frank thought less and less about Iowa as the business grew. For the second time in his married life, he built a house for his family, this time in Cherry Run Valley, eight miles from Titusville. And this time they moved in.

The house was spacious—three large rooms that included a living room with an alcove at one end, a family bedroom with trundle beds for two-year-old Ida and her three-month-old brother William, and a bright, cozy kitchen. The house was connected to the tank shop by a covered passageway. There Ida played, occasionally falling asleep in the mounds of fragrant pine shavings that covered the shop floor.

"My first reaction to my new surroundings," wrote Ida years later, "was one of acute dislike. It aroused me to a revolt which is the first thing I am sure I remember about my life—the birth in me of conscious experience."

She missed her grandfather's farm—the family popping corn and making maple sugar at the huge stone fireplace, the daily romps among the farm animals. The sounds of turkeys, ducks, and chickens were strangely absent, and even the occasional bark of a dog was almost drowned out by the din coming from the engine houses. More important, she was no longer the center of her grandparents' undivided attention.

Life in the oil region was different. Where grass had grown only a few months before, the ground was now covered with oily muck. There was an oil derrick in the front yard, but unlike the workmen who climbed up and down the maintenance ladder, Ida was not permitted to go near it.

Just beyond the derrick was a fast-rushing stream, bubbly and inviting to a two-year-old. Whenever she got close enough to watch the water splashing against the banks, her mother shouted a warning: "Ida! You're too close to the stream." Or, as she moved back toward the house, "Stay out of the oil! Stay away from the well."

With childish curiosity the little girl sat for hours on the footbridge tossing bits of grass, twigs, and stones into the rushing water below, and watching. Some objects floated; others sank.

One day, she tried the same experiment on her baby brother. Without realizing the seriousness of what she was doing, she shoved him into the stream and watched satisfied as his billowy skirt floated him on the water. Fortunately, the frightened baby screamed loud enough to attract a nearby workman, who snatched him from the waist-deep water before he sank.

Another time, Ida announced that she was "going back to Grandma." A half century later Ida told the story:

I knew the way the men went when they walked away from the shop, and I followed . . . but not far. Across the valley in which we lived ran an embankment. To my young eyes it was as high as a mountain and the nearer I came the higher it looked, the higher and blacker. And then suddenly as I came to its foot I realized that I had never been on the other side, that I did not know the way to Grandma's. I knew I was beaten, and sat down to think it over. Never in all these years since have I faced defeat, known that I must retreat, that I have not been again that little figure with the black mountain in front of it, a little figure looking longingly at the shanty dim in the growing night but showing a light in the window. Finally I turned slowly back to the house and sat down on the steps.

Eventually the door opened.

"Why, Ida! I thought you had gone to Grandma's," said her mother.

"I don't know the way," Ida answered in a quiet voice, tears streaming down her face.

"Very well. Come in and get your supper."

After that, nothing further was said.

The safety of two small children was only one of Frank Tarbell's worries. He had been in business for less than a year now and there was already a sudden decrease in the oil supply. Several of the largest wells had stopped pumping. Would he never have any luck?

Fortunately his fears were unwarranted. By April, 1861, the oil region was booming as never before. In fact, one well was shooting gushers of oil more than a hundred feet into the air!

Along with the new excitement came tragedy. Oilmen, not realizing the dangerous flammability of gas vapor from the wells, often left their lanterns burning nearby.

Then one night they learned a frightening lesson, when just such a lantern caused the explosion of the famed Rouse well, one of the area's greatest producers. In the fire that followed, eighteen bystanders and the owner of the well were killed. A badly burned survivor, eyes swollen shut and face charred, staggered to the Tarbells' house.

There were no hospitals in the newly established community. Instead, neighbors took care of one another in time of need. The Tarbells quickly gathered bed quilts and feather comforters for a makeshift mattress. In a few minutes the living room alcove became an emergency treatment center.

Frank and Esther gently removed the man's scorched clothing and applied linseed oil to his burns. For weeks Ida watched her parents care for him, changing bandages, propping him up with feather pillows. Finally, as his burns healed and the pain subsided, he was able to return to his work in the oilfields.

Soon after that, with the tank business flourishing, the Tarbells saved enough money to move their growing family—Ida, Will, little Sara, and the new baby, Frankie—away from the derricks and debris to the green hillside above. From the new house Ida could look down on the drilling activity in the valley below or look up instead at the changing beauty of the trees and shrubs—the oaks and maples, the mountain laurel and azalea. It seemed to Ida that the valley itself had grown quieter. Or was she simply noticing the noise less?

Soon she knew. Once again more and more drillers were finding dry holes along Oil Creek. The spectacular-flowing wells were drying up. Business at the Tarbell Tank Shop grew worse each day, and now her father talked about closing down and moving to Iowa.

Then, in January, 1865, the sudden news of another oil strike swept the valley. Already speculators and adventurers were pouring into the new fields about ten miles north at a place called Pithole. There was an unbroken line of travelers plodding through the muddy ruts in the valley, men on horseback and many on foot, moving alongside wagonloads of supplies and equipment. Many were recently discharged Civil War veterans, still in uniform, with guns and knapsacks slung over their shoulders.

Frank Tarbell, too, saddled up the family's horse, Flora, and joined the procession northward. At Pithole he found men hammering together a wooden city in the midst of green pastureland. Those without housing pitched tents or slept on the bare ground sheltered only by the trees. Men, soaked with oil that shot out of the ground, were hurrying to lease property.

Not a man to overlook opportunity, Frank Tarbell moved his tank shop to Pithole. With a partner, he also bought an oil lease nearby. From then on, each day he rode Flora back and forth along the heavily wooded path between the tank shop and the house in Rouseville. He carried a gun for protection against thieves who often waylaid passersby, but luckily he never had an occasion to use it.

Every night, just before dark, Ida would wait at the top of the hill, watching her father put Flora in the barn. Then he would bound up the hillside path and scoop the eight-year-old up into his arms. Father and daughter had grown close since the tiny Ida had hidden behind her mother's skirts on Frank Tarbell's return from Iowa.

One day in the spring of 1865, as Ida and her mother waited, they saw him coming up the hill, walking haltingly, his head drooping. Esther started down the path toward him. "Frank, Frank, what is it?" she called. Ida, too far away to hear his reply, saw that her mother was sobbing when she turned, holding her apron to her face.

Later Frank called the family together and explained that President Abraham Lincoln had been shot while attending a play in Washington, D.C. A day later, when news came of the President's death, the Tarbells placed a black crepe on the door in mourning for the great man.

Why all this sorrow for a man they had never met? the little girl wondered. The incident, tucked away in the back of her mind, marked the beginning of Ida Tarbell's lifelong fascination with Abraham Lincoln.

But there was little time to ponder tragedy in the outside world when there was so much tragedy nearby. A neighbor woman hurrying to build a fire in her cookstove had overlooked a live coal in the firebox and poured oil on top. In the flash fire that followed, the woman, together with two friends who tried to save her, burned to death.

However horrible this event, death was no stranger to mid-nineteenth-century families, who often stood by helplessly as a loved one died. Many parents watched their children struggle against contagious diseases for which there was neither prevention nor cure. The Tarbells were no exception.

When the youngest Tarbell, Frankie, became ill with scarlet fever, a dreaded childhood disease at that time, they could do nothing but wait and hope. His sister Sara had contracted it first and was recovering. Frankie, however, was growing worse.

Tears in her eyes, Ida stood outside the parlor door listening to the sobs of her anguished parents. She heard the doctor explain there was nothing more he could do, nothing at all. Little Frankie died.

For the rest of the family life went on. Orders poured into the new tank shop. To keep up with the increased business, Frank hired an extra clerk and eight new workmen. It was customary in the mid-1800's for an employer to provide room and board for his unmarried employees. Thus, the Tarbells built a bunkhouse for the men, all of whom were bachelors.

Having grown up on a farm where hired men lived close to the house and ate at the family table, Esther Tarbell knew exactly how to handle the situation. With the same firm discipline she had used in the classroom, she told the men she would not tolerate swearing, drinking or rough manners—even though she conceded that such behavior was commonplace in Pithole.

Many times, while visiting friends who lived on the hillside overlooking Pithole, Ida had listened to the goings-on in the town below—the profane shouting, ribald singing, and raucous laughter emanating from the saloons and dancehalls frequented by heavily rouged women and drunken men. These were the sights and sounds of a boomtown, the excitement of devil-may-care speculators who had no roots and wanted none. When the oil boom ended, they would simply move on.

Responsible businessmen like Franklin Tarbell, who wanted to raise their children in a law-abiding community, were willing to work to create a better life. Joining with others like themselves, they formed vigilante committees and petitioned for civil authority to bring about "the suppression of disturbances and scenes of immorality enacted in the streets every day, the destruction of the gambling tables which block the thoroughfares and at which youths . . . can be seen betting every day . . . robberies are perpetuated [sic] nearly every night and no man when he retires at night is confident of waking up the next morning with his life and pocketbook."

Even though the Tarbells were Presbyterians, they helped build the Pithole Methodist Church because most of the residents were Methodists. Now, for the first time in her life, Ida went to church, to Sunday school, and to Wednesday night prayer meeting. When traveling preachers staged religious revivals, she went every night of the week.

This new experience—sermons and lectures on conscience and morality—moved Ida to think about sin. "Often when I'm saying the polite and proper thing," she told herself, "I am thinking quite differently." This, she decided, was sin. Later, discovering that she wasn't the only person who hid unspoken thoughts beneath what was said aloud, she became a bit guarded and wary of others.

Life was busier now. Once a week Ida took piano lessons from a music teacher who had recently moved to the community. The Tarbells bought a beautiful piano, and each morning before school—to please her parents rather than herself—Ida practiced five-finger exercises until she played well enough to accompany the family's group singing.

And there were trips: short ones just beyond Cherry Run Valley and longer ones to neighboring states. Once they traveled by train to Cleveland, the bustling port on Lake Erie and one of the fastest-growing cities in Ohio. Passing the outskirts, the Tarbell children stared at the newly built oil refineries that were changing the city and the countryside, just as the derricks back home were changing the look of the hills of western Pennsylvania. In the center of Cleveland, the Tarbells visited well-stocked department stores, which were unlike anything they had ever seen in Rouseville.

At other times, the family went on "all-day excursion picnics." Ida's favorite picnic spot was Chautauqua Lake, about fifty miles from home. To get there, they took the train north to Mayville, New York, and there boarded a small white steamer that zigzagged across the lake, stopping at several locations along the shore to load and unload picnickers.

Will helped his father carry the picnic baskets to a shady spot near the water. While their mother spread a white cloth on the soft green grass, the girls opened the picnic baskets. Ida set out the tin cups and plates, the new steel forks and knives, and Sara carefully folded the well-worn cloth napkins, placing one next to each fork.

From the baskets they took sliced veal loaf and cold tongue, hard-boiled eggs, buttered rusks—enough for two apiece—spiced peaches, cucumber pickles, chowchow relish, cookies, doughnuts, and Mrs. Tarbell's special picnic cake.

By the time the steamer whistle sounded the return trip, the children had full stomachs and were exhausted from chasing butterflies.

3

A Young Lady of Titusville

Shortly after Ida's thirteenth birthday, the Tarbells were able to leave the house on the hillside at Rouseville and move to Titusville to enjoy the advantages of the larger city. Although it was the site of the oil rush that had followed Colonel Drake's well, Titusville was no boomtown. In fact, local residents saw the excitement as a temporary inconvenience which would soon disappear.

They pointed out proudly that Titusville was a lumber town founded more than twenty years before anyone thought of drilling for oil. Old folks still speaking with the accents of their homelands recounted tales of persecution and famine in the Old Country and taught their children to cherish the freedoms of their adopted land. These hard-working souls, with memories of hardship in Scotland, England, or Germany, were proud of the town they had built in the wilderness and vowed that no man would disrupt their orderly community.

When the oil commotion began in 1859, thousands of strangers had rushed to Titusville—drillers, brokers, roustabouts, draftsmen, surveyors. As in Pithole, some were quick-money men with no allegiance to the community, ready to move on to better hustlings at a moment's notice. But others, like Frank Tarbell, established businesses in the area and brought their families to settle permanently. Many of their descendants still make their homes in Titusville.

Back at Cherry Run, Ida had attended a small private school in which all grades were taught by one teacher. Teacher and students were close friends, who visited each other's homes frequently.

Public school was different. Not only was the teacher a stranger, but for the first time Ida sat in a crowded classroom filled with boys and girls she had never seen before. Looking around the room, she decided that the teacher didn't even know she was there. To prove her point, she let the others go to school the next day, while she took her lunch and an armful of magazines to the edge of town. There she sat down on the grassy bank of Oil Creek and spent the day reading.

The following morning, before classes began, the teacher called Ida to her desk and asked for an absence excuse. Jolted, Ida admitted she hadn't any. With that, the teacher rapped on her desk for class attention and in front of everybody lectured the new pupil on the evils of truancy.

Ida's face reddened, but beneath her embarrassment she was secretly pleased. The teacher had noticed her absence! From that day on she not only attended class regularly, but she listened and studied. By the end of the school year Ida was first in her class.

School was exciting. Ida enjoyed math puzzles and "guess-the-word translations." After fourteen weeks of zoology, geology, chemistry, and botany, Ida was finding answers to questions that had been in her mind ever since she began collecting stones and insects near Cherry Run. Now her collections seemed not only beautiful and interesting, but for the first time she saw the relationships that exist in nature.

In the new house Ida no longer shared a room with her sister. Her room—the "tower room" she called it—was set apart from the rest of the house, at the top of a steep staircase. The tower had large double windows set into three of the four walls, making the room bright and airy. There Ida had her desk, her collections, and a microscope purchased with her savings.

Typical of Frank Tarbell's ingenuity, the handsome house, which still stands today, was unique. When the wells at Pithole had dried up and the town was abandoned, Ida's father had bought one of its finest buildings —a hotel called the Bonta House. It was especially admired for its verandas, its fine iron brackets, and its elegantly finished woodwork. A few days after the sale, Frank and several hired men carefully dismantled the hotel, bracket by bracket, molding by molding, and from this treasure came the Tarbells' new home. Christmas that first year in Titusville was more than Ida had ever dreamed possible. She thought back to the Christmases in the little house behind the tank shop and remembered sitting on the cold floor threading popcorn for the pine tree that her father had cut in the woods nearby. How many times had she heard her mother say, "Wait, just wait; the day will come."

In those days her gifts had always been the same—nuts and candy. Now, as her mother promised, the day had truly come. They were living in a beautiful new house with, in Ida's words, "a gorgeous Christmas tree and a velvet cloak for me—and a fur coat for my mother. I hadn't the slightest idea what there was for the rest of us, but those coats were an epoch in my life—my first notion of elegance."

Titusville was growing more cosmopolitan and affluent every day. A new opera house was almost finished, and the main street was being graded to provide a suitable track for trotting fine horses. Businessmen, to impress their associates, told of personal meetings with powerful railroad men from the East who were showing interest in local oil shipments. Titusville took on a new air of gentility as it matured into a prosperous city, confident of its role in the nation's oil industry.

Then something went wrong. Several oil refiners from Cleveland, Pittsburgh, and Philadelphia, calling themselves the South Improvement Company, began buying up small refineries and combining them into larger, more efficient plants.

Under the leadership of John D. Rockefeller, the South Improvement Company reorganized to become the Standard Oil Company, which in a few years' time would grow into a giant monopoly, controlling every phase of the oil industry except drilling.

At first, Pennsylvania's oilmen took little notice of the growing company—until it affected them personally. Suddenly, independent producers found themselves unable to sell their oil unless they were willing to accept whatever price the company's refineries offered them.

Rumor was that Standard Oil had worked out a private agreement with the railroads, which allowed them a special low rate for shipping their oil. Not only that, but allegedly the railroads agreed to rebate to Standard Oil a portion of the shipping charges paid by other shippers.

Other oilmen claimed the railroads were keeping the company informed of their entire shipping schedules and the names of their customers. Armed with the information, Standard Oil could therefore move in, offer the customer a lower price, and put the independent out of business.

Whatever their methods, legal or illegal, the fact remained that Standard Oil products—kerosene (the earlier spelling "kerosine" was no longer used), lubricating oil, paraffin—were cheaper than anyone else's. Consumers, of course, chose the lower-priced products, and Standard Oil grew bigger and more powerful.

Independent oilmen were furious. Standard Oil was ruining them, driving them out of business. Their only choice was selling out to the company—if the company wanted to buy—or going bankrupt. Titusville was in an uproar of emergency meetings and stormy speeches protesting the company's monopoly. There were nightly torchlight marches. Railroad cars loaded with the company's oil were overturned, the oil dumped on the ground. The company's buyers were evicted bodily from the oil exchanges where buyers and sellers of oil met to transact their business.

The independent oilmen called on their senators and congressmen in Washington, urging them to pass an interstate commerce bill which might prevent the company's monopolistic activities. They traveled to the state capitol at Harrisburg and appealed to the Pennsylvania legislature for help. Even small producers like Ida's father and his partner joined with other independents in refusing to sell to Standard Oil. Caught in a financial bind and unable to pay his bills, the partner shot himself, leaving Frank liable for his debts.

Night after night Ida watched her father sit stern and silent. He no longer played the Jew's harp while his children sang. Instead he spoke seriously with his wife. From family friends who had chosen bankruptcy rather than selling out to Standard Oil, Ida heard judgments which branded the company "sly, greedy, and unethical." At fifteen she was learning about injustice.

In the outside world, however, women were not supposed to worry about such matters, much less do anything about them. An intelligent, ambitious girl might someday become a teacher, but any career in government, law, or economics was reserved exclusively for men. Yet, as she grew older, Ida found herself increasingly drawn to these areas and to the growing struggle by women for the right to be heard.

In 1868, when Ida was eleven years old, the Fourteenth Amendment to the Constitution had granted all *male* Americans equal rights under the law. A cry of female outrage swept the country. Women worked long hours in coal mines, on farms, and in factories. Why should they not vote, too? Susan B. Anthony and Elizabeth Cady Stanton organized groups to protest discrimination against women and to demand equal rights under the Constitution. The year 1872 saw the first try for the American presidency by a female candidate. No men took her seriously at the time, but Victoria Woodhull, brilliant speaker and women's rights advocate, was in deadly earnest.

Back in the 1850's, Amelia Bloomer had begun campaigning for reform in women's dress. She advocated wearing a practical, even if ugly, short skirt over loose trousers gathered at the ankles. This costume, called bloomers, was often worn by women who campaigned in the suffrage movement.

When suffrage-movement speakers came to Titusville, Ida and her mother attended their lectures. As Ida heard and read more about woman's role in America, she decided on the rights most important to her: the right to an education and the right to economic independence. Winning those rights, however, would be a lot harder than donning a pair of bloomers. Ida stuck to her petticoats and decided to go to college and become a teacher in biology. She had heard that Cornell, a college in the hills of western New York, had been admitting women for the last four years. It seemed like a good place to try.

Then one Sunday shortly after she had made her decision, a certain Dr. Lucius Bugbee stopped by to have dinner with the Tarbells. He was charming, entertaining, and persuasive. He was also president of Allegheny College, a Methodist institution, about thirty miles away.

As the dinner-table conversation came around to Ida's plans, Dr. Bugbee added some comments of his own. Was Ida aware that Allegheny College had begun admitting women two years before Cornell? Here, he added, was a "pioneer opportunity" for a young woman interested in the advancement of her sex. If the few colleges that had opened their doors were to keep them open, if others were to imitate their example, two things were essential: women must prove they wanted a college education by supporting the schools in their vicinity; and they must prove by their scholarship what many doubted—that they had minds as capable of development as those of young men.

Before Dr. Bugbee left the Tarbell parlor Ida had decided to enroll at Allegheny, the only woman in a class of forty "hostile or indifferent" men. She was nineteen years old. Many girls of her age in Titusville were already married and raising children, but Ida was set on a course that would take her far away from Titusville and the mores of her time.

4

From Co-ed to Headmistress

In the fall of 1876 Ida, gray-eyed, tall and majestic-looking, seemed in cool possession of herself as she boarded the train that was to take her to college. Actually, she was shy and a bit afraid as she traveled the thirty miles from her home to Meadville, Pennsylvania, where Allegheny College was located. The town, only a few miles from the Ohio border, had grown up on the banks of French Creek, one of the Allegheny River's many tributaries.

Local residents boasted that George Washington stopped there in 1753 while en route to Fort Le Boeuf. They pointed out the exact spot where he drank the clean spring water that poured from the hills. A few of the town elders remembered the stories told them by their parents about the Indians and the French and British soldiers who had fought to gain control of northwestern Pennsylvania.

Many of the original settlers had come from distinguished New England families who had helped establish America's earliest colleges. It was only natural, therefore, that they should found a college at Meadville. To their children they explained that men who seek to build a democratic nation must have a center of learning where they can study their responsibilities and learn to think clearly. Friends and relatives who remained in New England contributed large sums of money to finance the construction of buildings. They collected books to fill the shelves as fast as they were built. Thus began Allegheny College.

In 1876, when Ida Tarbell first walked onto the college campus, she saw Bentley Hall, a building in the colonial style, and as beautiful as Philadelphia's Independence Hall. Ida would never forget her first sight of that plain but classic frame building, visible through an arch of trees. It was then the men's dormitory. Directly in front of her stood Ruter Hall, a rectangular brick building which housed classrooms on the lower two floors and a library on the third. There were no living quarters for women on the campus.

Ida spent many hours each day in the library. Surrounded by rare volumes from the famous publishing houses of Europe and the tons of books from New England that had been shipped overland in wagons, she found a new kind of companionship. Whenever she wasn't attending classes, she would curl comfortably on a window seat overlooking the town and its surrounding hills in the distance and read.

Even though six years had passed since Allegheny College opened its doors to women, only ten had enrolled to date. True, the Fourteenth Amendment to the Constitution had started people thinking about the status of women, but many more years would pass before large numbers of women entered America's colleges. Ida Tarbell was the only co-ed in the freshman class. There were no female sophomores, and only two juniors and two seniors.

One day soon after classes began, Ida walked down the path in front of Bentley Hall and crossed the soft green lawn to sit and study in the shade of the trees. But her pleasure was interrupted when she looked up from her books to see one of the senior women waving and shouting at her: "Come back, come back quick. You must not go on that side of the walk; only men go there."

Despite such restrictions for women, or perhaps because of them, Ida worked harder than most men students.

The classrooms were lit by kerosene lamps and heated by potbellied stoves made of cast iron. There were no desks, only straight-back chairs grouped near the stoves. During the long winter, Ida's ankle-length dresses dragged heavily through the snow and in the warm classrooms clung wet against her legs.

However, she forgot her discomfort the moment Professor Jeremiah Tingley walked into the classroom. A witty man of fifty and the chairman of the natural science department, Professor Tingley conducted his classes with a good humor that made everyone relax. He recalled his own student days, reminiscing about the time his teacher held up "a round, water-washed stone" and asked him to report on it. He explained how he examined it, turned it over in his hand but could see nothing to report. Then he paused, staring into the palm of his hand while the class waited for the rest of the story. With that introduction Dr. Tingley brought out a binocular microscope and told the students, "It is not the outside but the inside of things that matters."

One afternoon Dr. Tingley called the student body together in a special session to tell them about a new invention recently exhibited at the 1876 Centennial Exposition in Philadelphia. "You'll talk to your homes from these rooms one day," he told the group. "New York will talk to Boston." The boxlike instrument he held in his hands was a homemade model of a telephone.

Often in the evenings, professors and students got together for discussions, stimulating talk about politics, economics, and ideas in general. A new world was opening up to the young woman from the oil region.

Years after she left college Ida credited her Latin teacher, Professor Haskins, with teaching her discipline, the trait which most characterized her work in later life.

George Haskins, a scholar of ancient history, was stern and demanding. When students were careless and unprepared with class assignments, or even if they seemed disinterested in how the Romans contributed to our civilization, he turned on them, bitter and caustic. Ida, accustomed to people who accepted one another's shortcomings graciously, was so jolted by his brusqueness and fearful of his contempt that she always did her best. She kept regular study hours, forcing herself to steady, dogged work, even on topics she disliked. Throughout her life this routine remained a habit.

"If I failed at any point in this discipline," she later admitted, "I suffered a certain mental and spiritual malaise, a dissatisfaction with myself hard to live with."

Perhaps it was this devotion to her work, as much as her intense independence, that kept her from marrying. Her goal in life was a successful career, and none of the pleasant young men who escorted her to concerts and meetings could change her mind. Marriage was not in her plans.

By the time Ida graduated from college in the spring of 1880, she had already signed a contract for her first job. The following spring she became headmistress of the Poland Union Seminary in eastern Ohio, at the very adequate salary of five hundred dollars a year! With such a salary, she hoped to save enough to go to Europe for further study with a world-renowned biologist.

Poland, Ohio, was a five-hour train ride from Titusville. As Ida described it:

It had the air of having been long in existence, as it had. Here there was no noise of railroads, no sign of the coal and steel and iron industries which encircled it, but never passed its boundaries. Here all people seemed to me to live tranquilly in roomy houses with pleasant yards or near-by farms where there were fine horses and fat blooded sheep, and where planting and harvesting went on year in and year out in orderly fashion.

Poland's only industry, if one could call it that, was the seminary. For thirty years, local residents bragged that the daughters of "the best families" came to Poland to be educated. The retiring headmistress, Miss Blakeley, had long been revered for her fine personal qualities and her skill as a teacher. Now the word spread through Poland that Miss Blakeley was being replaced by an inexperienced and very recent graduate of Allegheny College.

During her first two weeks as headmistress, Ida heard of nothing but the high standards and fine work of Miss Blakeley. To a less determined young woman, it would have been unnerving, but Ida worried less about her own shortcomings than she did about the job that faced her. Until now, she had not fully understood the challenge facing the seminary and the new headmistress.

For the first time in its history, the seminary competed for students with the new—and free—public schools. Mr. Lee, the seminary president, advertised widely that the seminary, unlike public schools, offered each individual student whatever specialized training she desired. Few parents knew, however, that this individualized teaching rested solely on the headmistress. Mr. Lee, of course, was too busy with administrative matters to assist with the teaching.

Ida taught two classes in each of four languages—Greek, Latin, German, and French. That wasn't all. She also taught geology, botany, geometry, trigonometry, a class in what was called verb grammar, and another in "percentage arithmetic."

In addition, she continued the seminary's practice of offering refresher courses to teachers who taught at other schools in the area. These teachers, older and more experienced than Ida, came to the seminary year after year and reviewed the subjects they taught. But each time they came, they used the same textbooks and the same problems, until many teachers had simply memorized answers to questions without mastering the principles involved. Realizing this, Ida selected problems from new books. Although several teachers resented the change, they soon understood that the young headmistress did not mean to embarrass them, but simply wanted to help them learn.

Every night Ida fell into bed exhausted. She had no time for her microscope. Even worse, she wasn't saving any money. Her entire salary, which had looked like a fortune when she signed the contract, barely paid for room and board. But how could she quit? What would her friends say if she failed at her first job?

She decided to stay on. At the end of the second year she was in debt and more than ever overwhelmed by her job. Embarrassed and disappointed that she couldn't help herself, she asked her father for a loan to pay her bills. Then she resigned as headmistress.

Regardless of the difficulties at the seminary, Ida certainly had not wasted her two years there. Through her dealings with students, teachers, and townspeople, she had learned a great deal about people and their problems. In the countryside around Poland, she was witnessing at first hand the changes in American farm life as industry pushed in closer on farmers whose forebears had cut away the forests and established themselves on the land. Clinging to the dreams of their fathers before them, these people hoped one day to see their sons work the family farm.

But times were changing rapidly. The farmlands south of Lake Erie were giving way to industry. Coal mines and slag heaps scarred the hills; mills and factories fouled the green meadows and pasturelands. The breezes blowing in from the Great Lakes could not clear the air of its new load of smoke and soot. Young people, no longer interested in farming the family land, went to work in new industries where they could earn a salary.

Ida watched new settlers come into the area. Thousands of immigrants, fleeing poverty and oppression in eastern Europe, sought work at the iron-ore smelting furnaces only ten miles from Poland. They came from the old Poland, from Hungary, and from Czechoslovakia, bringing new customs and languages unknown to the farmers whose own grandfathers had come from Britain or Germany. Underpaid and unable to speak English, the newcomers were ready to face the dangers and hardships of the coal mine or the smelting furnace.

Once, a furnace burst open, pouring molten metal on the workmen nearby. But the fear of unemployment was greater than the fear of accident, and the workers were always ready to return. They were hired from day to day and never knew when they would be out of work. Often during business slowdowns, the mills shut down operations without giving advance notice to their employees. More than once, Ida saw crowds of angry men and women shrieking protests and pounding at the locked gates that circled the mill.

Ida packed away her memories of Poland, Ohio, and moved back to Titusville.

5

A New Career

Going home was not without its pleasures. There was comfort in having one's family under the same roof and sharing the same dinner table. But for a grown woman, educated and self-reliant, the loss of independence was galling. No longer was Ida's tower room a place of sanctuary where she could be alone with her microscope. Now she shared it with her sister Sara's dolls and playhouse.

Several months after Ida returned home, another dinner guest changed her life. The Tarbells, with their customary hospitality, had invited Dr. Theodore Flood, a prominent local clergyman. Dr. Flood, recently retired from his church duties, was now editor of *The Chautauquan,* a small magazine published in Meadville, Ida's former college town.

It was interesting work, Dr. Flood told the Tarbells, but really too much for his small staff. Then, turning to Ida, he asked if she would like to help for a month or two in a new department they were establishing.

Without hesitating, Ida agreed.

The Chautauquan was the official publication of the Chautauqua Literary and Scientific Circle, a four-year home-study course which marked the beginning of America's adult-education movement. To Ida, the mention of Chautauqua brought back memories of family trips to Mayville and picnics by the Chautauqua Lake. The Tarbells, together with several other families had even purchased a small piece of land, and had built a cottage there for summer use. Over the years, a summer community had grown up, devoted to lectures and discussion groups as well as to the usual summer pursuits. The movement had begun with Bible instruction, but in time the programs broadened to include the important scientific and intellectual topics of the day. Famous musicians gave concerts, and well-known personalities came to speak. Chautauqua was fast becoming a cultural center that attracted people from all over the country.

Because most adults at Chautauqua—or anywhere else in the United States—had never gone to college, they were eager to learn what they missed. The next step, therefore, was a home-study course that could be mailed anywhere.

The Chautauqua directors planned carefully. They wrote out lesson plans and selected the best books available, such as Green's *Short History of the English People,* a textbook often used in college courses. The new program was called the Chautauqua Literary and Scientific Circle.

Men who were busy farming their land, workers who labored in the nation's new industries, and particularly women who had been barred from higher education simply because they were women subscribed eagerly. In less than a year, eight thousand people were enrolled. Five years later there were twenty thousand, and by the time membership reached its peak there were a hundred thousand.

By 1880, the organization was circulating a monthly magazine which contained portions of required readings and lists of supplementary references.

This was *The Chautauquan,* the magazine edited by Dr. Flood. Now, two years later, it was expanding its services. Many study-group members—particularly those in the Far West, isolated in tiny mountain towns and remote farm communities—had questions about the reading material, but no study aids. There were few libraries. Encyclopedias and even dictionaries were scarce at that time, so members directed their questions to *The Chautauquan.* Letters would come in from everywhere—from steelworkers in Cleveland, from farmwives in Kansas—asking such questions as "How do you pronounce 'pedagogue'?" "Who was John Locke?" "What does 'conciliation' mean?"

To Dr. Flood, the methodical young teacher from Titusville seemed the ideal choice for handling the problem. Ida's new job was to anticipate these questions by preparing detailed notes to accompany each lesson. Because her assignment required only two weeks' work each month, she enrolled at her alma mater, Allegheny College, for work toward a master's degree.

As time allowed, she visited Meadville's well-stocked libraries and gathered the necessary information. Working carefully, double-checking each date, name, event, and even pronunciations, she drew up explanatory paragraphs that were short, informative, and easy to read.

The work was tedious, and she worried about her accuracy: "What if the accent was in the wrong place?" "What if I brought somebody into the world in the wrong year?" Occasionally, there would be a slipup, and *Chautauquan* readers who knew how to use reference books were quick to point up the error.

Ida may have had little enthusiasm for her new work, but she was learning to be a journalist. No longer did the printer's special language sound odd and unfamiliar. When he said "galley," Ida knew he wasn't referring to a medieval war vessel but to the oblong tray that held the set type. And when he said "the dummy," he meant the columns of printed material pasted on a sheet exactly as it would appear on the magazine page.

Because *The Chautauquan's* staff was small, Ida often filled in wherever she was needed—handling correspondence, proofreading, writing a few paragraphs, and occasionally running sheets through the printing presses. The more she learned, the more the editor-in-chief asked her to do.

One day he stopped at her desk to explain plans for the magazine's further expansion. In the future, he said, *The Chautauquan* would contain more literary criticism, excerpts from editorials published in leading newspapers, and articles dealing with travel, politics, science, and art. Then, after commending her work, he asked if she would accept appointment as associate editor.

This was exactly what Ida wanted—an opportunity to write articles about the ideas that flooded her mind. Already she was planning her first article—on woman's creativity.

I had been disturbed for some time by what seemed to me the calculated belittling of the past achievements of women by many active in the campaign for suffrage [Ida later explained]. They agreed with their opponents that women had shown little or no creative power. That, they argued, was because man had purposely and jealously excluded women from his field of action. The argument

was intended, of course, to arouse women's indignation,
stir them to action. It seemed to me rather to throw doubt
on her creative capacity. . . .

At the moment it was being said in print and on the
platform that, in all the history of the patent office, women
had taken out only some three hundred patents.

Ida found this unbelievable and untrue. She knew too
many women who were brilliantly ingenious—on the
farm, in the kitchen, or wherever their roles in life had
taken them. Ida's enthusiasm for her subject obscured any
fears she may have had about her ability to write a full-
length article. Although she never mentioned it, her main
concern was whether or not the editor-in-chief would
permit a woman to handle an assignment out of town.
He never hesitated, however, and a week later she was at
the United States Patent Office in Washington, D.C.

There, in the first few days of searching, she located
over two thousand patents issued to women. After interviewing the director and noting his comments on women
inventors, she wrote her story. A month later it appeared
in *The Chautauquan*, complete with her by-line.

Each summer the magazine's Meadville offices closed
down. The staff packed their equipment and moved to
summer quarters on the shores of Lake Chautauqua,
where they published *The Daily Herald*, an eight-page
newspaper distributed early each morning to summer
visitors.

Ida's assignment—two columns of editorials every day—
brought her interviews with the important people who
came to speak or teach; "men who were stirring youth and
shocking the elders by liberal interpretations of history
and economics."

Although an interview never lasted more than thirty minutes, she prepared with her usual thoroughness, first reading the person's biographical material, which was on file in the director's office, and then hunting through old newspapers and magazines for any mention of his name. Then she wrote out a list of questions to ask.

Even so, her first interviews were clumsy. She was shy, and fearful of not doing the job well enough to meet her own exacting standards. Once, while talking to a member of the President's Cabinet, her hand shook so much that she lost her place on the list of questions and asked the same thing twice.

Because she wanted to be accurate, she wrote down every word of every answer of her first interview, only to discover that she had recorded pages of "ands" and "buts." Naturally, she was exhausted. Even worse, she couldn't remember anything about the person's appearance because she hadn't had time to look at him.

Never one to repeat a mistake, however, Ida improved with each interview until she was able to throw away her question sheet and take down only important comments.

For six years she worked on *The Chautauquan*. For the first time since her college graduation, she had enough money to live comfortably, and, even more important to one who treasured independence, her future seemed secure. She had grown a bit plumper and more matronly, in the past years, and she wore her straight dark hair smoothly piled high on her head.

However, she was growing restless. The work was pleasant, but it had become routine. Perhaps the pleasantness might make her satisfied, she thought, and then she would be trapped. What had seemed so important a few years before was no longer so. With her master's degree attained and almost a decade of work experience behind her, she was a different person. Interest in her microscope had disappeared. Now she wanted more than anything else to write about people, about their attitudes and actions.

Ida had been born just before the Civil War. That was only a little over thirty years ago, but what changes had taken place in that time! The bitterness that followed the war continued to divide the country. The devastated South was trying to recover, while its black citizens tried to find their way in a hostile America.

In the North and West, industry was making strides as never before, its power concentrated in the hands of a narrowing circle of businessmen. A growing web of railroads linked the Atlantic and Pacific coasts. Large industrial combines were growing too, based on such essentials as railroad transportation, oil, iron and steel, coal, and meat packing. The frontier was almost gone. Men who would have sought their own land a generation ago now went to work for others in the growing cities. A few got richer, many poorer, and discontent seethed just below the surface.

In her thirty years, Ida had lived through several economic crises—inflation when the dollar bill bought less and less, followed by depression when people lacked money even for food. Surely economic problems, too, are man-made, she thought.

Now the United States, completing its first century of independence, was face to face with the worst labor disturbances in its short history. Violence, born of discontent with low pay and dangerous working conditions, swept through the coal mines, the copper mines, and the steel mills. Railroaders in the West, replaced by Oriental laborers who worked for less money, massacred an entire Chinese community in Wyoming.

Newspapers reported mob actions, reprisals by management, shootings, destruction of property in all parts of the country, even in small towns. Strikers battled militiamen in the streets of Pittsburgh and in West Virginia coal towns. On several occasions federal troops, called to restore order, moved into Pennsylvania, New York, and New Jersey. People talked of "the bloody 1880's," of anarchists, Communists, and "chaos in the cities."

Ida's notebook was filled. Originally she had intended to use the notes as a basis for a novel. Now she found herself more interested in the questions they raised: Was there a science of society just as there was a science of botany? What lessons did history teach us?

Always her thoughts came back to her own relationship with the ever changing world. To find herself, she decided, she must learn more about others—particularly women who had lived and worked before her.

The French Revolution had taken place a century ago, and Ida found herself fascinated with the women who worked at the forefront of the movement. She admired especially Madame Roland, the party leader and writer who stood bravely before the guillotine and proclaimed her belief in freedom.

Ida Tarbell was thirty-three years old when she decided to leave *The Chautauquan,* go to Paris, and write. "I wanted freedom," she later said, "and I had an idea that there was no freedom in belonging to things, no freedom in security. It took time to convince myself that I dared go on my own."

Paris was the cultural capital not only of Europe, but of the Western world. Poets, politicians, artists, and musicians of many nations were drawn there. It was a big jump from Meadville to Paris, but Ida felt it had to be done if she was to grow as a writer and as a person.

To those who knew her, nothing seemed more improbable. For one thing she was shy, especially among strangers, and in 1890 an American woman did not just "run off" to Europe by herself. Even more improbable was her plan to become a free-lance writer. Except for her limited experience on *The Chautauquan,* she knew nothing at all about getting her material published.

Thoughts of the future crowded all other considerations from her mind. If there were important lessons to be learned abroad, lessons that could benefit her fellow Americans, she wanted to learn them. She contacted newspaper editors in Chicago, Cincinnati, and Pittsburgh, asking if their readers would be interested in reading about the French way of life. They agreed to read her material, nothing more.

One morning Ida appeared at her editor-in-chief's desk.

"I'm leaving," she announced. "I'm going to Paris."

The editor was shocked. "How will you support yourself?" he asked.

"By writing," said Ida.

In complete disbelief, he answered, "You'll starve. You're not a writer."

His words echoed her own growing doubts, but her mind was made up. If she didn't leave now, she knew she never would.

6

Paris: City of Light

The day Ida said her good-byes, two other *Chautauquan* staff members announced they were leaving their jobs to go with her. For them, however, the trip was to be a long vacation. They planned to pay their expenses with small but regular allowances from their families. Josephine Henry and Mary Henry were both from Titusville. Josephine, like Ida, was a graduate of Allegheny College. Mary, whom Ida thought beautiful, was the daughter of a militant worker in the Women's Christian Temperance Union.

A few weeks later, as the three young women boarded a ship anchored in New York harbor, another friend arrived, waving a freshly issued passport. Could she come with them? she asked. Happy to have another person share expenses, they welcomed her aboard. Ida was especially pleased. She had only $150 to last until she found an editor willing to buy her articles!

Paris in 1890, nicknamed City of Light and Capital of the World, was a mecca for artists, writers, and intellectuals, who frequented the sidewalk cafés and the galleries, museums, and theaters that lined the beautiful boulevards.

At that time all eyes were on the Paris World's Fair, which had recently opened. Paris sparkled with multi-colored electric lights that illuminated the city's monuments and public buildings and especially the grand attraction of the fair—the newly finished Eiffel Tower. The four American women from Pennsylvania were among the first who climbed its 750 steps to view the beautiful city far below.

Even before leaving Meadville, Ida and her friends decided they would rent an apartment in the Latin Quarter, a section of Paris situated on the Left Bank of the Seine River. There, in the bustling area near the Musée de Cluny, the famed museum filled with medieval treasures, they would live among students who were willing to get by with only bare necessities, in order to stay in Paris. Even today that part of Paris is crowded with students, hurrying from place to place on bicycle and on foot.

Apartments were very much alike—small, dingy rooms filled with well-worn furniture. If the women didn't actually see fleas or roaches, they convinced themselves that there were none. Most important, the rent was low, and the area fascinating.

On the Rue du Sommerard they found an apartment large enough for the four of them—two tiny bedrooms, a living room, and a kitchenette to be shared with Madame Bonnet's other roomers. Not quite like home, to be sure, but after all, one must make concessions in Paris.

Without waiting to unpack, the Americans hurried out to look around. They walked in and out of neighborhood stores, smiling and speaking the very correct French they had learned in college. Although their accents marked them as foreigners, they behaved like other customers, buying one sweet *croissant,* one hard roll, or one egg. Obviously, Parisians bought only exactly what they needed from day to day—a custom quite different from home, where everybody bought more than enough and expected to have leftovers.

Most of the tiny shops were run by women shopkeepers, whose husbands worked at jobs in other parts of the city. They were pleasant, but understandably reserved with strangers. When regular customers came in, however, the shopkeeper greeted them with hugs and a noisy display of affection. It was difficult to believe that in a few short weeks the Americans would be greeted with that same gusto.

Notebook in hand, Ida was already gathering information on life in Paris. No more sightseeing, she decided, until she had finished at least one article. Time was running out if she intended to eat and pay rent. By the end of the week, she had completed two short articles and sent them off to American editors. Then she rewarded herself with a tour of Paris.

Everything she saw and heard suggested an idea for an article: Why was Paris so much cleaner than American cities? Why did Parisians prefer to eat at tables set outside on the sidewalks? She sorted the ideas carefully, always remembering that a salable article had to interest American readers.

To the people she interviewed, Ida introduced herself as a journalist and student. This was justified, she reasoned, because she intended to be both, even though she hadn't sold any articles yet or enrolled at the Sorbonne, Paris's great university.

Each day brought new insights. Like many Americans of that day, Ida believed that the goal of all poor people was to get rich. Perhaps this was true in the expanding economy of the United States in 1890, where owning a business was synonymous with success. But it did not seem to be true in France.

The Frenchmen Ida talked with found satisfaction and dignity in their jobs without aspiring to any other status in life. They were proud people who found permanence in jobs that Americans considered only stepping stones to wealth or power.

Ida pitied the poor of Paris who were unemployed and unable to find jobs, no matter how menial. They spent their days dozing furtively in libraries, museums, and churches, and the cold nights walking the streets to keep from freezing. Often a charitable organization handed out bowls of hot soup to hungry passersby. These were the scenes Ida described in the articles she mailed to American editors.

In the Latin Quarter, Ida saw another class of poor, "the gallant poor," she called them, because they were too proud to admit they needed help. Most of them, beyond the usual employment age, lived on their meager savings or perhaps a small inheritance; others, simply on the generosity of friends.

"The Countess," as everyone called her, was typical of this group. Often Ida watched her, tall and erect, walking with the grace of a *grande dame* as she left the narrow house across the street. Her hair was carefully brushed and pulled back in a tight bun. Across her shoulders hung a once elegant silk cape, now faded and patched.

On several occasions late at night, Ida had seen the woman rummaging through rubbish cans, pulling out whatever usable items she could find.

One morning, while Ida was buying her breakfast

croissant, the Countess walked into the shop smiling and nodding to everyone there. The shopkeeper, obviously pleased with her visitor, quickly poured her a cup of coffee. "Will not Madame honor me by trying my coffee?" she asked. "It is still hot."

"If that will give you pleasure, my good Marie," answered the Countess.

The woman was hungry and the shopkeeper knew it, thought Ida.

After the Countess left, the shopkeeper turned to the American woman and explained, "It is an honor to have so great a lady come into one's shop."

Evidently aristocratic manners—*la grande manière*—were more important to the French than money.

Ida was writing about the Countess when the mailman delivered a letter postmarked "U.S.A." It was from the editor of the *Pittsburgh Dispatch,* announcing his acceptance of the article she had written the week she arrived in Paris. A check for five dollars was enclosed.

Within the next two weeks, letters arrived from the *Chicago Tribune* and the *Cincinnati Times-Star,* agreeing to buy what she had sent them. Thus Ida established a syndicate of three newspapers willing to run her articles on a regular basis.

Just before Christmas, *Scribner's,* one of America's leading magazines, sent a one-hundred-dollar check, payment for a character study of the elderly fabric dyer from Titusville who had tutored her in French conversation.

The sale to *Scribner's* proved an important point in journalism: Always choose a publisher who specializes in your kind of material. Ida's choice of *Scribner's* was deliberate; she knew they published articles with a French flavor.

After three months in Paris, the young writer had placed a story about the Eiffel Tower, another about a famous French anarchist, and a series dealing with Parisian municipal problems. She was confident that the money from her writing would be enough to cover her expenses. Just as important was the personal satisfaction of knowing that skeptical friends back home would see her by-lines.

Editors back home were beginning to notice it, too. When *Scribner's* editor Edward L. Burlingame made his annual visit to Paris, he climbed the four flights of stairs to Ida's apartment and asked about her future plans.

"I would like to write a book," she told him, "about the women of the French Revolution. I'm especially interested in Madame Roland. If I do a good piece of work, would your publishing house be interested?"

The editor, often asked this question by aspiring writers, tried to encourage her without committing his firm. "The suggestion would have to be considered in New York," he replied.

Not long after his visit, however, Mr. Burlingame sent a letter saying that his firm was indeed interested in the project and wanted to read the manuscript.

A short time later Ida heard from another American, Samuel S. McClure, founder of the McClure Newspaper Syndicate. He had read her two-thousand-word article describing a typical French government worker and promised to send her a ten-dollar check as soon as it appeared in print. More important than this acceptance, however, was the short note at the bottom of the letter suggesting that she try "a series of sketches of French women writers."

With this encouragement, Ida set up a writing schedule five days each week, which usually began at eight o'clock in the morning and didn't end until well after midnight. Soon she had completed twelve short pieces written carefully in very legible longhand, and sent them off to Samuel McClure.

As fast as one article went into the mail, she began another. For most people, such discipline would have been unbearable, but with McClure buying her articles, Ida worked herself to exhaustion and was happy.

Weekends were reserved for relaxation. If the weather was good, Ida and several friends, most of them American professors attending lectures at the Sorbonne, took short trips in and around the city. Sometimes they packed lunch and spent the day aboard a *bateau mouche,* a flat-bottomed boat that traveled up and down the Seine. Once they took a train to Versailles, where they visited the magnificent palace and the gardens built by King Louis XIV. At other times they might travel to the cathedral towns of Chartres or Rheims. When bad weather kept them indoors, the young people toured the city's museums and ancient churches.

Sunday belonged to Madame Bonnet, the landlady. That day everyone in the house was invited to her weekly dinner party—Ida, her three roommates, and the four Egyptian students who lived across the hall. The Americans knew nothing about the Egyptians except that one of them was a prince and that all four were, in Ida's words, "quite the most elegant-looking male specimens so far as manners and clothes went" that any of them had ever seen.

Chatting in French interspersed with a few English words, the group often talked far into the night, discussing their countries, customs, and religions. The visits gave Ida a view of other worlds that lay beyond America and

Europe. The Egyptians, in turn, were surprised by the four straitlaced young American women, who refused their invitations to go dancing on a Sunday because their religion would not allow them to. The prince and his friends shook their heads.

"*Très religieuses,*" they whispered among themselves.

By the end of Ida's first year in Paris, the Egyptians had returned home. So had most of her American friends, including her three roommates, who had completed their European sightseeing.

Ida was alone now. Without friends to share it, the little apartment on the Rue du Sommerard suddenly seemed big and empty. It was also getting harder to pay Madame Bonnet at the end of the month. Writing was slow, hard work, and even though Ida sold most of her articles, the five- and ten-dollar checks that trickled in from the publishers barely covered her living expenses. Worst of all, she would sometimes spend weeks on an article, only to discover that no editor wanted it.

Overwhelmed with homesickness, Ida turned to her family for comfort.

"You can't tell me too much of your daily doings," she wrote her mother. "I live off them."

In later years, Ida Tarbell would still remember herself as a lonely young woman in Paris, waiting for letters from home.

If they did not come regularly [she recalled], I scolded and wailed; I begged for details of their daily life. My mother was an intimate letter writer, delightfully frank about her neighbors and about the family, fretted because father spent so much time with his precious Sunday school class of girls, described every new frock, told what they had for Sunday dinner, announced the first

*green corn in the garden, the blossoming of her pet
flowers. . . . Occasionally she would apologize for her
homey details, particularly after I had written a long
guidebookish epistle home describing some ancient monument I had been visiting.*

It seemed to be the story of the Poland Union Seminary
all over again. She was doing a good job, she had worked
hard, but she simply could not make a living. Lonely
and discouraged, Ida thought of going home.

Then one day in the early summer of 1892, a slender
young man came bounding up the four flights of stairs to
the Tarbell apartment, taking the steps two at a time. It
was S. S. McClure himself. He was passing through Paris
and had written Ida, asking for an appointment.

"I've just ten minutes," the young man announced
breathlessly. "Must leave for Switzerland tonight."

Ida just stood and listened as McClure described his
early struggles and aspirations, how he finally became a
publisher. Now he was about to launch a popular magazine called, appropriately enough, *McClure's Magazine*.
The ten minutes stretched into two hours, and McClure
finally explained he wanted her to do a series on the
achievements of great French and British scientists.

Before Ida could reply, he was on his way out the door.
"I must go," he said suddenly. "Could you lend me forty
dollars? It is too late to get money in town, and I must
catch the train for Geneva."

"Certainly," said Ida, never thinking to refuse him. She
had put aside forty dollars for a vacation in Europe, and
now she handed the money to this stranger.

"How queer that you should have that much money
in the house!" said McClure.

"Isn't it?" answered Ida. "It never happened before."

Ida never expected to see her money again, but less than a week later, McClure's London office sent her a check for the amount.

Immediately, Ida began work on the new assignment and forgot about returning home. Recalling the great scientists whose work she had studied in college, she chose to begin with Louis Pasteur, the chemist who told the skeptical world about tiny organisms, too small for the eye to see, that lived in the air.

The name of this man had given the world a new word, "pasteurization," which described his process of using heat to destroy objectionable organisms that caused foods to sour and carry dangerous infections. People all over the world were grateful to Dr. Pasteur for the inoculations he had developed which prevented rabies, and the French particularly honored him because he had found a way to prevent silkworm disease, thereby saving the French silk industry.

After wondering what she could say to men like Pasteur, Ida admitted later: "It took all my courage to talk with these gentlemen, but I was soon to find they were the simplest and friendliest of people."

She arrived at the Pasteur Institute exactly on time for her appointment with its distinguished director. The elderly Pasteur and his wife lived in an upstairs apartment furnished with heavy furniture, thickly woven draperies, and dark, soft rugs, fashionable at the time.

Louis Pasteur was then seventy years old. His left side had long been paralyzed by a stroke, and he moved with difficulty. He spoke haltingly, pausing between phrases, but his eyes were bright and alert as he welcomed Ida.

After she explained the series of articles she was doing

for S. S. McClure, Ida asked if the Pasteurs had any photographs for illustrations. Mrs. Pasteur took out their old albums, dating from childhood, and for several hours the three sorted pictures while the elderly pair reminisced about the past.

When Ida noticed the Pasteurs growing tired, she thanked them and ended the interview. Dr. Pasteur walked with her to the door. Then, shaking her hand warmly, he cautioned, "Be careful. The stairway is very dark."

After Ida's article appeared in the second issue of *McClure's*, in September of 1893, she took a copy to the Pasteurs. The visit was not intended to be an interview, but looking at this kindly old man who had given the world so much she could not resist asking if he had any thoughts or advice he would like published in the magazine's "Edge of the Future" section, in which leaders from science, industry, religion, and literature were asked to contribute a paragraph or two "embodying their convictions as to the outlook for the world's future. . . ."

Dr. Pasteur sat down at his desk in the library, picked up his pen, and wrote: "In the matter of doing good, obligation ceases only when power fails."

7

The Biographer

Samuel McClure, pleased with the science series, offered Ida several new assignments. So did *Scribner's*.

Reasonably certain of these two markets, Ida sought no others. With the extra hours she visited the National Library, reading letters, books, and papers which contained bits of information needed to piece together the life of Manon Roland.

Walking back and forth to the library, Ida paused to look at the house where Manon was born and grew up. As her mind wandered back to the days of the French Revolution, she imagined the young woman looking down from her window at the scene she herself now saw—the Seine, the statute of King Henry IV, the slow-moving traffic crossing the Pont-Neuf, Paris's most famous bridge.

Not far from there, Ida passed the building which once housed a goldsmith shop owned by Manon Roland's father, and farther along, the church where she had received first communion.

Hurrying by the Conciergerie, the prison where the outspoken woman had awaited execution, Ida's pace quickened. She made her way to the Place de la Concorde, where Madame Roland stood before the screaming mob and shouted her famous words: "O Liberty! What crimes are committed in thy name!" A few seconds later the guillotine silenced her forever.

Looking at the silent buildings around her, Ida thought about the history they had witnessed—the struggles for freedom, struggles against leaders to whom power was more important than the welfare of the people.

"How could I understand Madame Roland until I understood the elemental force which for centuries had been sweeping Paris in big and little gusts? . . . It looked at the moment as if I were going to have a good opportunity to watch a revolutionary revival—of what proportions no man could tell."

Even now, Ida saw signs of political strife and dissatisfaction in Paris. Someone had thrown a bomb into the Chamber of Deputies, wounding two deputies and eighty spectators sitting in the gallery. There were constant threats of violence against the government because of unpopular decisions surrounding the United States' involvement in building the Panama Canal.

Frequently, university students trying to bring their grievances to public attention protested in the streets. On one occasion women students at the Sorbonne wore skimpy costumes to the annual Beaux Arts Ball, and as a result the Chamber of Deputies proposed legislation prohibiting such behavior.

The students, enraged that their freedom of dress should be restricted, formed long lines, one hand grasping the hand of the person in front and the other grasping the hand of the person behind, and ran through the streets of Paris chanting, "Down with the puritans!"

Cafés were jammed inside and out with noisy youths, some so unruly that police were called to disperse them.

By the next day the crowds of demonstrators grew larger as onlookers joined in. An innocent bystander was killed, struck on the head by flying debris. Suddenly, people were running and screaming. At the sound of broken glass, shopkeepers, experienced with such outbreaks, pulled down heavy wood shutters to protect their storefronts.

As in many riots, the original cause was forgotten when hoodlums joined in the excitement and used the situation to loot and destroy. The protest which had begun as a student demonstration ended in wanton destruction.

Horse-drawn omnibuses were overturned in the streets and used as barricades. For a week, the rioters rampaged through Paris until soldiers, some on foot, some on horseback, were called in to assist the police.

Slowly the violence subsided, and life went back to normal: carpenters repaired damaged buildings; shops opened their doors to customers; homeowners replanted their trampled gardens.

Pondering the riots, Ida wondered if humans were innately violent: If man is rational and civilized, what causes him to lose control of himself?

On this score she even had second thoughts about Madame Roland. Without realizing it, Ida had idealized her heroine's role in history. Now, the more research she did, the more real Madame Roland became—and the more disappointing.

The facts about Madame Roland were becoming clear: While admirably outspoken in the cause of freedom, she was personally ambitious, highly opinionated and a bit shallow. She was involved with the Girondists, a political movement headed by her husband, Jean Marie Roland de la Platière, which for a time seized control of the government. Once in power, they neglected the problems of oppressive taxation and food shortages that tormented the common people and chose instead to divert the country's attention by encouraging a war with Austria.

Officially, it was Madame Roland's husband who headed the country's policy-making council, but in practice it was Madame Roland who dictated the council's policies. She wrote her husband's speeches and letters, many supporting the goals of rich property owners rather than the needs of the people.

There were many political factions in France at that time, each vying for control of the government. Revolution and counterrevolution continued until Madame Roland became a victim of the Girondists'—and her own—bad decisions.

With her heroine's motives open to question, Ida had misgivings about completing the book. She might have ended her research right then except that a friend, knowing of her project, introduced her to Madame Marillier, the great-granddaughter of Monsieur and Madame Roland.

Every Wednesday evening, Madame Marillier, a kind, gracious woman—*la bonne madame,* a Frenchman would say—invited a group of Sorbonne professors to her home. Over pastries and coffee the guests, all of them historians and political scientists, discussed their country's past and heatedly debated its future. Pleased and flattered by Ida's interest in her great-grandmother, Madame Marillier invited her to join the group.

During her first meeting, Ida sat quietly, listening to the rapid exchange of French and watching the intensity of the participants. Feeling like an intruder, foreign and suspect, she was nevertheless drawn with fascination to French political life. Week after week she attended these sessions until eventually she challenged opinions and argued with the same fervor as the others.

Delighted with Ida's understanding of French history—and greatly impressed that her articles were appearing regularly in the American press—Madame Marillier introduced her to the special manuscripts librarian in charge of the Roland collection at the National Library. The librarian took the collection from safekeeping and opened it to Ida, who was the first person, other than family members and library staff, to have access to the materials.

In the spring of 1893, Madame Marillier invited Ida to be her guest at LeClos, the country estate in southeast France which had been in the Roland family more than a century before the French Revolution. Manon herself lived there for four years after she married Jean Marie Roland.

According to Madame Marillier, the château had not changed since then. Even the grape growers and wine makers worked as they had under Madame Roland's direction.

To reach LeClos, the two women traveled from Paris by train, arriving in Villefranche, a small country town, where they were met by a farmer driving a horse-drawn cart. For more than an hour they bumped along narrow, dusty roads, past orchards and vineyards, until they finally stopped in front of a heavy wood gate, the only opening in a yellow stone wall which bordered LeClos.

Once past the gate, the women rode toward a white château with a red tile roof and high towers on each corner. At one side was a large open courtyard; on the other, carefully trimmed formal gardens. Far beyond, barely visible in the distance, were snowcapped mountains which stretched across France to meet the Swiss Alps in the east.

Inside, servants prepared dinner at a huge open fireplace in the kitchen. The clean-scrubbed stone floor did not show the wear one might expect. On the walls hung Madame Roland's copper kettles, which were still in use.

There was a game room, floored with brick, set aside for billiards. The heavy table, hand-carved, with ornate designs, was the only piece of furniture. On the walls were guns and emblems which had belonged to successive generations of French soldiers.

The living room—*le salon*—was both a music room and a library. There was a piano at one end of the room, and shelves of books covered the other. Portraits of family members looked down on furnishings upholstered in yellow plush.

Gesturing toward the books, Madame Marillier explained that many had belonged to the Rolands and perhaps contained hand-written notations that Ida would find interesting. Also, suggested her hostess, why didn't she search through the old desks and bureau drawers for papers and letters still hidden there?

Knowing that such research is tedious, Madame Marillier interrupted every few hours and insisted that they stroll in the gardens or down past the grape arbors.

Wherever they walked, there were workers tending the chores of the huge estate—trimming shrubbery, hoeing vegetables, tending grapes. Madame stopped frequently to introduce her guest. "Mademoiselle Tarbell comes from the same country as your vines," she said, pointing toward the grape arbors. To Ida, Madame Marillier explained that American vines had replaced French varieties that had been devastated by plant lice. Thus the workers held the United States in esteem—even though few knew where it was located.

Finally, her research completed, Ida returned to Paris. As far as she knew, she had read everything Madame Roland had written that was still in existence, and everything anyone else had written about her.

Now, with her notes spread out in front of her, she was disappointed. Instead of a clear-eyed innocent who fought the evils in society, Madame Roland emerged as a calculating politician, wishy-washy in her loyalties, who encouraged violence to achieve her goals.

As Ida herself explained:

I had undertaken the study of this woman in order to clear up my mind about the quality of service that women could give and had given in public life, particularly in times of stress. I had hoped to come out with some definite conclusions, to be able to say "the woman at this point will be a steady, intuitive, dependable force. She will never lend herself to purely emotional or political approaches to great social problems; she knows too much of human beings. Her business has always been handling human beings. Building families had been her job in society. You can depend upon her to tell you whom to trust, whom to follow, whom to discard . . . and she will be no party to violence. She knows that solutions are only worked out by patient cooperation, and that cooperation must be kindly. . . . She has a great inarticulate wisdom

*born of her experience in the world. That is the thing
women will give" . . . that is what I hoped to find Madame
Roland giving.*

Instead, Madame Roland's life negated such ideas.
With this disappointment, Ida's interest in the women of
the French Revolution disappeared.

Nevertheless, *The Life of Madame Roland* was almost
ready for the publisher—if she could find one.

*Never did I so realize my ignorance of life and men
and society as in the summer of 1894, when I packed up
the manuscript of my life of Madame Roland to take it
back to America. . . .*

*Of course, I told myself, I would go through with it.
I would put down what I had found as nearly as I could,
even if I had not got what I came for. And then came the
question, Can I get what I came for? Is it to be found—the
real answer to my question about woman in society, the
point or position where she can best serve it? Can I find
an answer to this other question that has so disturbed me
—the nature of revolution?*

8

The Historian

Once again Ida was practically penniless. *McClure's* had not paid for the science series because, like other American businesses after the Panic of 1893, they were caught in the depression's money squeeze.

She had no choice except to go home; but without money, even that was impossible. Looking through her possessions, she chose the only item of value, her sealskin coat, and took it to the nearest pawnbroker. His loan, plus the few francs tucked away in her desk drawer, was enough for ship passage.

Convincing herself that the trip was a vacation, she daydreamed of returning to Paris as a recognized author, housed in a Latin Quarter *salon* overlooking miles of tiled rooftops, where the world's most interesting people —writers, painters, intellectuals—would gather for late evening discussions.

For now, however, after four years in Paris, she planned to visit her family, put the final touches to her book, and then travel leisurely to New York City, where she would show the manuscript to Scribner's.

No sooner had she arrived in Titusville, in June of 1894,

than her plans changed. There was a letter from S. S. McClure asking that she come immediately to New York City and begin work on a biography of Napoleon Bonaparte.

A few days later, Ida walked into the offices of *McClure's Magazine*. They were on the sixth floor of the building and appeared informal and crowded. With only a perfunctory greeting, S. S. McClure handed her a letter from Gardiner Green Hubbard, a collector of Napoleon portraits and papers. Many people recognized Mr. Hubbard as the father-in-law of Alexander Graham Bell, inventor of the telephone, but few were aware of his important collection.

The letter granted *McClure's* permission to reproduce for publication whichever items they selected. What S. S. McClure needed at this point was a solid text to carry the Hubbard material. Ida, he felt, could provide such a text to his, and to Mr. Hubbard's, satisfaction.

Ida could not understand why an American magazine would want to publish a series of articles about Napoleon. Perhaps French readers would be interested, but American readers—never! The decision, of course, rested with S. S. McClure, and he was willing to pay forty dollars a week if she would begin immediately.

Thus Ida Tarbell became a staff member of *McClure's*. Forty dollars was a high salary in those days, especially for a woman. The average working woman, bent over her sewing machine in a dressmaking sweatshop, might be earning no more than four or five dollars a week.

The situation was unusual even for a magazine, which usually paid for an article, and not for the time taken to research it. But S. S. McClure was no ordinary publisher. He was determined to have the best available talents and the best available articles, and to get both, he was ready to pay his writers for their time and trouble. To Ida, Mc-Clure's policy meant the financial independence she had sought for so long.

The next mail brought a personal letter to Ida from the Hubbards, inviting her to Twin Oaks, their summer estate in Washington, D.C. The estate, considered one of the finest, was several miles north of the White House, near Grover Cleveland's home.

In the 1890's, Washington was a growing city, with a population exceeding a quarter of a million. The streets now stretched northward beyond the original site of the city, into the low hills. There, spacious homes with wide lawns lay hidden among ancient elms, pin oaks, and maple trees.

Pennsylvania Avenue, the town's best-known street, stretched from the executive mansion, nicknamed the White House in the early 1900's, to the Capitol, which sat on the brow of a hill overlooking the Potomac River. The towering Washington Monument, completed little more than a decade before, was the city's Eiffel Tower.

Unlike Paris, Washington was new and sprawling. There were no old palaces, no antique shops, no hidden streets.

When Ida arrived at Twin Oaks and the butler opened the door, she saw before her the most beautiful home she ever had set eyes on. Informed of their guest's arrival, the Hubbards came into the hallway to introduce themselves and to welcome her. Mr. Hubbard, who was over seventy years old, was wiry and energetic; Mrs. Hubbard, a bit younger, restrained and dignified.

Occasionally, Samuel McClure dropped in unannounced from New York, bringing proofs of the Napoleon prints and, without asking his hosts' permission, spreading them over the entire floor. Embarrassed by her editor's brashness, Ida apologized to the Hubbards. Mrs. Hubbard laughed and assured her there was no need for apology. "That eagerness of his is beautiful. I am accustomed to geniuses," she said, obviously referring to her son-in-law.

Surprisingly, one could find almost as much information about Napoleon in Washington as in Paris. A complete file of his correspondence was available at the State Department. There was a voluminous collection of books, pamphlets, and papers at the Congressional Library, now called the Library of Congress.

For six weeks Ida came daily to the library, where she worked for long hours at a small writing table set between the stacks of books.

By the time the first Napoleon article appeared in print, she had finished the second. To her amazement *McClure's* was receiving letters from readers commending the article.

"I expected nothing for myself from it more than the forty dollars a week, and the inner satisfaction of following the thrilling drama from the terror of '93 down to St. Helena," Ida later recalled. "That satisfied me. But to my surprise I did get the last thing in the world I had expected, the approval of a few people who knew the field."

One of the most favorable comments came from a prominent American who traced his family back to Napoleon—Charles Bonaparte, later Attorney General of the United States under Theodore Roosevelt. He invited Ida to have lunch with him.

With the second installment, the series gained popularity. As a result, the circulation of *McClure's* increased. In

1895, the articles were published in book form and by 1898, over a hundred thousand copies had been sold. Forty years later, Ida was still receiving royalty checks, but even then she was unable to understand her readers' interest. All she could say was, "There must have been something in his [Napoleon's] characterization of 'living'."

Noting her success, Scribner's now asked that she finish polishing *The Life of Madame Roland*. They were ready to publish. S. S. McClure, too, was urging her to accept a new assignment—a series on Abraham Lincoln. *McClure's*, he pointed out, had "overlooked the most vital factor in our life since the Civil War, the influence of the life and character of Abraham Lincoln."

Now was the time to do the story, said McClure, because the great man was dead only thirty years and there were many people still alive who had reminiscences not yet recorded.

By this time Lincoln's papers, particularly his letters and speeches, had been collected and published. Volumes dealing with almost every phase of his life were also available. Best known of these were *Abraham Lincoln: A History* and *Complete Works of Abraham Lincoln*, by Lincoln's secretaries, John G. Nicolay and John Hay.

What, if anything, remained to be written?

Ida went to talk to John Nicolay. Lincoln's one-time secretary eyed her suspiciously. "You are invading my field," he said. "If you write a popular life of Lincoln, you will decrease the value of my property."

Taken back by his attitude, Ida assured him, "If I can write anything that people will read, I am making readers for you."

Realizing that "Lincoln was his whole life," Ida pointed out that Nicolay was no different from the rest of us who feel displaced "when the time comes that our field is invaded by new workers. . . . We may put up a 'no trespassing' sign, but all to no use."

Unlike Nicolay, who saw Lincoln through the eyes of those who made history with him, Ida planned to begin her story among the farmers of Kentucky and Illinois. These were the sons and grandsons of families who, like the Lincolns, had come over the mountains from the east to settle in the river valleys of the Ohio, Cumberland and Mississippi. They had shared the same struggles and worked the same land. There were old men who still remembered Lincoln as a young woodsman, storekeeper, and country lawyer. Using their impressions as background for presenting published documents and, if possible, stories and recollections of the man himself, Ida Tarbell hoped to produce an adequate history.

No matter what had been included in previous histories, there was always the possibility of finding a few letters or photographs that had been overlooked. Perhaps there were old stories hidden away in county histories or yellowed newspaper clippings.

On a frigid day in February 1895, S. S. McClure accompanied Ida to the railroad station, where they waited for the train that would carry her to Illinois. As she boarded, he shouted last-minute instructions: "Look! See! Report!" Then, with sudden concern for her comfort, he added, "Have you warm bed socks? If not, we'll send you some."

Ida sat back in her seat, dozing, as the rhythm of the train continued monotonously. Her thoughts went back three decades as, once again, she saw her father come up the path, walking haltingly, her mother running toward him, shouting, "What is it, Frank?" She remembered the black crepe on the door and her childish confusion at "this sorrow for a man we had never seen, who did not belong to our world."

Now she knew why the world had mourned Abraham Lincoln. What she didn't know, however, was that she was beginning work on one of history's great Lincoln documents—*The Life of Abraham Lincoln*. Later published in book form, it was to be reprinted many times, and it is still available at libraries throughout the world.

In Chicago, Ida stopped to talk with President Lincoln's son Robert. As she sipped a cup of tea, she studied the man's face and mannerisms, but could see no resemblance to his roughhewn, angular father.

Robert Todd Lincoln, a plump man, perhaps fifty years old, radiated well-groomed freshness and an air of assurance. Although he had been Attorney General of the United States under Presidents Garfield and Arthur, and Minister to the Court of St. James under President Harrison, he had only an academic interest in politics. Instead, he was a successful businessman.

Despite his friendliness, Robert Lincoln had little information to offer. He simply reaffirmed Ida's opinion that the presidential papers would be of no value because they had been thoroughly covered by Nicolay and Hay. Then, almost as an afterthought, he mentioned a portrait, a daguerreotype never published, possibly the earliest picture of his father in existence.

When Ida saw it, she knew she had the illustration for the first installment of her series. Here was a Lincoln never pictured before. It was the portrait of "a young dreamer," clear-eyed, without sadness, neither shabby nor ungainly.

Carefully she tucked the picture into her briefcase and headed for Kentucky. There her search continued until she had accumulated more than three hundred pieces of unpublished material. From observations and interviews, she reconstructed the physical appearance of Lincoln's homes and the sites of his most important appearances.

She sought out people who had worked with Lincoln in Illinois before his climb to the presidency. She interviewed many others who had heard him speak. A few still remembered the year 1858, when Lincoln, running for the Senate, attacked slavery in a series of historic debates with his opponent, Illinois Senator Stephen A. Douglas. Those debates were to bring Lincoln to national attention. Now, thirty-seven years later, those who had been there could still describe the quality of his voice, his mannerisms, his physical appearance. Some repeated stories he had told.

Occasionally at the conclusion of an interview, someone would say, "Well, those were good speeches, but they were nothing like the 'Lost Speech.' That was the greatest thing Lincoln ever did."

Judge Scott of Bloomington, Illinois, who had heard Lincoln deliver the "Lost Speech" at the first Republican state convention ever held in Illinois, told Ida, "Unless one heard that speech he cannot know what eloquence is."

Another man who attended told her, "It has been so universally regarded as a masterly speech and the effect of it upon the convention was so wonderful that I fear no report of it can be given to the public that would do justice to Mr. Lincoln or give a proper conception of the speech and of its remarkable power and eloquence."

These recurring comments whetted Ida's curiosity so much that she began asking questions. The speech had been made in 1856, two years before the famous debates.

A newspaper reporter told her that to his knowledge there were no written accounts available. Even the reporters, he said, were so moved they forgot to take notes.

Knowing reporters, Ida couldn't accept the man's story. Yet after interviewing several others who said the same thing, she was more curious than ever. Finally, someone told her that at least one man—a Massachusetts lawyer named Henry Whitney—had taken notes. Mr. Whitney, active in Lincoln's campaign, had been with him in Bloomington on May 29, 1856, the day of the speech.

Ida took the next train to Massachusetts.

Yes, said Mr. Whitney, he had notes, and she was welcome to read them. With that, he brought out a bundle of yellowed papers. It was that simple.

Using Mr. Whitney's notes and personal recollections, Ida compiled a version of the "Lost Speech"—Lincoln's first public stand against slavery.

Back she went to Illinois to show it to people who had heard Lincoln that day. Everyone agreed she had indeed captured the main arguments and the spirit of his presentation. In fact, many recognized Lincoln's actual phrases, taken down verbatim by the Massachusetts lawyer.

Borrowing the words of witnesses, Ida wrote:

There stood Lincoln in the forefront, erect, tall and majestic in appearance, hurling thunderbolts at the foes of freedom, while the great convention roared its endorsement! . . . As he described the aims and aggressions of the unappeasable slaveholders and the servility of their Northern allies as illustrated by the perfidious repeal of the Missouri Compromise two years previously, and their grasping after the rich prairies of Kansas and Nebraska to blight them with slavery and to deprive free labor of this rich inheritance, and exhorted the friends of freedom to resist them to the death—the convention went fairly wild. It paralleled or exceeded the scene in the revolutionary Virginia convention of 81 years before when Patrick Henry invoked death if liberty could not be preserved.

McClure's Magazine published Ida's version of the speech. As the Lincoln articles continued to appear, Ida continued with her research, learning to distrust official histories, challenging accepted tales that had little or no basis in fact, drawing a thoroughly human portrait based on documentation and eyewitness accounts. She had started by writing a biography, but she was learning an important lesson in journalism.

9

The Journalist

Ida's interest in Abraham Lincoln brought troublesome thoughts about American history. Pondering the aftermath of the Civil War, when there was so much "greed and hate and indifference to the sufferings and rights of others," she asked herself, "Did war as a method of righting wrongs so loosen the controls which man in times of peace establishes over himself that he is incapable of exercising the charity, the peaceful adjustments for which Lincoln called?

". . . True, this war had ended slavery as a recognized institution, given the black man legal freedom, but how about opportunity, discipline for freedom? And then again, was a war necessary to destroy slavery? Was it not already doomed? Lincoln thought so. Doomed because it was showing itself unsound economically as well as because it outraged man's sense of justice and humanity."

Drawn to the problems of her country, particularly at a time when there was talk of another war, Ida no longer thought of returning to France. Instead, with McClure's consent, she now moved to Washington, D.C., where she could study and report firsthand on current issues.

Ida contacted the Hubbards, her friends since publication of the Napoleon articles. Through the Hubbards, who welcomed her back as "one of the family," she met Alexander and Mabel Hubbard Bell, who lived just across the street.

Whenever the Hubbards and Bells entertained—as they frequently did—Ida was included, and thereby given the opportunity to meet Washington's diplomats, statesmen, and scientists.

At Mrs. Hubbard's suggestion, Ida moved into a rooming house on I Street between Ninth and Tenth. The neighborhood was good, although not quite as desirable as a few years before, when each brownstone had housed only one family. Nevertheless, at this address lived the eminent leader of the Republican party, Massachusetts Senator George Frisbie Hoar.

The house, beautifully furnished and immaculately clean, was managed by the elderly widow of a prominent physician. The rooms were spacious and comfortable, the meals excellent, and the company pleasurable—especially during Sunday morning breakfasts.

Not only did the landlady make the best codfish balls and coffee in Washington, but Sunday breakfast was the one time each week when Senator Hoar put aside his usual formality and entertained the diners with long recitations. His sonorous voice, dramatic and clear for a man almost seventy years old, filled the room with passages from classical literature, particularly the writings of Homer and Virgil. Occasionally, in a lighthearted mood, he regaled his listeners with New England anecdotes.

Ida's workdays began early and ended late. As a working reporter, she attended important government functions and met regularly with Cabinet members, department heads, and other officials who were making American policy decisions.

In 1896, she attended her first Washington inauguration, watching William McKinley, onetime graduate of Allegheny College, take the oath as twenty-fifth President of the United States.

Less than a year later, pressure began building toward war with Spain. On February 16, 1898, as Ida was interviewing General Miles, Commanding General of the United States Army, at Army-Navy Headquarters, an orderly rushed in and reported breathlessly: "Two hundred fifty-three unaccounted for, two officers missing, ship in six fathoms of water, only her mast visible, sir!"

The U.S. battleship *Maine* had been blown up in Havana Harbor.

The explosion was caused by a submarine mine, but no one knew how it had happened or who was to blame. Nevertheless, some of the most powerful American newspapers, eager for war, were quick to pin the responsibility on the Spanish government.

During the next two months, Ida visited General Miles frequently. Congress and the nation's military leaders pushed toward war. Often, Theodore Roosevelt, then Assistant Secretary of the Navy, hurried through the halls "like a boy on roller skates" as he planned the role of his Rough Riders.

That spring, in April of 1898, the United States declared war on Spain. Many, but not all, were in favor of the conflict. The mood of the nation turned somber and *McClure's*, like other magazines, turned its attention to the clash between the two nations in Cuba and the

Philippines, which were part of Spain's colonial empire. By December 1898, however, the fighting was over, and the United States had gained control not only of Cuba, but also of Puerto Rico, Hawaii, the Philippines, and a whole string of smaller islands. America had started on a new course of foreign influence and expansion, and although some voices were raised in protest against that policy, most people were content to go along.

The country, at peace again, was enjoying a new prosperity, but it was a prosperity enjoyed by a comparative few. Jobs were more plentiful, but the wages remained low. On the other hand, business profits soared as increasing numbers of smaller companies combined into large corporations known as trusts. Stifling competition, the trusts extended their influence into every phase of American life, including steel production, railroads, meat packing, electrical supplies, coal, glassware, and farming tools. The financial returns to those heading the trusts were of course enormous—especially in the absence of an income tax. By 1901, it was estimated that 1 percent of the population controlled 54 percent of the nation's wealth.

An early antitrust law had been passed in 1893—Ida's friend and fellow boarder Senator Hoar had worked for its passage. But the law simply remained on the books, unused and therefore ineffective.

Nevertheless, discontent was growing within the country, and that discontent was finding its way into the popular press. The magazines especially were in a strong position; they provided entertainment and information at a time when movies, radio, and television were still far in the future. New high-speed printing presses made it possible to turn out, in a short time, thousands of glossy issues featuring striking photographs, many of them in color. Selling for as little as ten or fifteen cents a copy, they quickly reached and influenced a mass market. By the late 1890's, there was a growing number of such magazines, but *McClure's* remained one of the leaders in the field, with half a million readers.

One of the reasons for its success was Samuel McClure's unerring instinct about what would interest the reading public. *McClure's* had built up its following through biographies such as those about Napoleon and Lincoln, through fiction by writers such as O. Henry and Rudyard Kipling, through exclusive stories about the latest inventions. In 1899 Samuel McClure sensed the new spirit of reform, and he called his staff together.

In addition to Ida, there was Ray Stannard Baker, a Michigan journalist who had covered early labor disturbances for a Chicago newspaper. He also loved to write short stories, which was how he had found his way to *McClure's*.

There was Lincoln Steffens—a native of California and a product of schooling in his home state and at European universities. A former police reporter and one of the finest journalists of the day, he was a friend of Theodore Roosevelt. Although originally hired as managing editor of *McClure's*, Steffens soon found himself back in the field, turning his searching eye on the problem of corruption in the cities of America.

Finally, there was John S. Phillips, the associate editor and an invaluable friend, coordinator, and administrator.

Together, these journalists made up what was perhaps the finest staff of any among the popular magazines. Now *McClure's* was to turn its attention to trusts and monopolies. Discussing the approach most likely to interest the

public, they decided to highlight one of the most powerful trusts of the time—the Standard Oil Company.

Standard Oil and John D. Rockefeller had come a long
way since the days of the South Improvement Company.
In addition to its hold on the refining of petroleum,
Standard Oil controlled railroads, banks, utilities, and
life insurance companies.

Ida suggested a complete history of Standard Oil, a detailed picture of its methods of operation, and its effects
on the country. The logical staff member for this assignment was of course Ida herself. No one was more qualified. Born just before the Pennsylvania oil rush, she had
grown up among the derricks and refineries. She still
remembered what had happened in 1872, when the railroads and the outsiders from the South Improvement
Company tried to seize control of the industry. Later
she called it her "first experience in revolution." She had
only a vague idea as to how Standard Oil completed its
takeover, but she remembered what she called "the hate
and suspicion and fear that engulfed the community."
And although a score of years had passed—she had been
fifteen years old at the time—she remembered clearly
the day her father's business partner, driven to financial
ruin, shot himself, leaving her father to pay off his debts.

Now, as she boarded the train for Titusville, where she
would begin her research, she realized the intensity of her
feelings and determined that her articles would be documented history, nothing more.

First she turned to the records of congressional and
state investigations, the voluminous transcripts of sworn
testimony taken from years of court proceedings against
Standard Oil. She interviewed people who remembered
the events of the 1860's and 1870's, and wherever pos-

sible, she dug out old agreements, court files, and correspondence. Although most people were willing to talk about Standard Oil, inevitably they warned her, "*McClure's* has courage, but if you go ahead they'll get you."

Franklin Tarbell, too, hearing of his daughter's assignment, cautioned her to give it up. "Don't do it, Ida," he said. "They will ruin the magazine."

"Nobody thought of such a thing in our office," Ida explained. "We were undertaking what we regarded as a legitimate piece of historical work. We were neither apologists nor critics, only journalists intent on discovering what had gone into the making of this most perfect of all monopolies."

In a few weeks, back in McClure's New York office (her work on the magazine had made necessary a move to that city), Ida's desk was heaped with documents which she sorted and indexed. The mass of material went back to 1872 and included everything she could find through 1900.

One file contained contracts; another, newspaper clippings; and a third, detailed reports and comments. Nowhere in all this information, however, was the one report she wanted most—the transcripts from an 1872 federal investigation of the South Improvement Company. That investigation had forced the company out of business. Soon afterward, however, Standard Oil took its place. Presumably, this report documented the company's earliest attempt to secure special rates and rebates from the oil-bearing railroads.

Wherever Ida inquired, people told her the same story: "You'll never find a copy. They have all been destroyed."

But once a document is printed, persistent searching will turn up a copy somewhere. Ida was convinced of that. When she finally located copies in each of two private collections, both owners refused her permission to read them. Eventually, however, her persistence was rewarded. In a file of old letters, she found the entire investigation reprinted in pamphlet form.

Another time, seeking another piece of this jigsaw puzzle of Standard Oil's history, she tried to find a copy of the important New York State Hepburn Investigation in 1879 of the railroads and industries. She was told by no less an authority than the librarian of the New York Public Library that "only a hundred copies were ever published. It is a scarce piece. I've known of a complete set selling for one hundred dollars. Years ago it was understood that several important railroad presidents whose testimony was given before the committee bought up and destroyed as many sets as they could obtain."

One month later Ida located a copy that the search-and-destroy committee had overlooked. Now, with all the major documents in her possession, she was ready to write.

In the meantime, stories about the persistent Miss Tarbell had reached the ears of officials at Standard Oil. Who was this woman and just what was she up to? To find out, they sent a literary man—Mark Twain, author of *Huckleberry Finn* and *The Adventures of Tom Sawyer*, and one of the foremost writers of the day. In what appeared to be an accidental meeting, Twain approached S. S. McClure. He explained that his good friend, Henry Rogers, a Standard Oil executive, had asked him to inquire about Ida's work.

"You will have to ask Miss Tarbell," McClure answered.

"Would Miss Tarbell see Mr. Rogers?" asked Twain.

Ida readily agreed. From her point of view, nothing

could be better. It was one thing to read about Standard
Oil but quite another to meet face-to-face with a member
of the company.

She wasn't optimistic about the results, however. Earlier
attempts to meet with company officials had failed, yield-
ing only "formulated chatter used by those who have
accepted a creed, a situation, a system, to baffle the in-
vestigator trying to find out what it all means." She
wondered if Mr. Rogers would speak candidly.

Early in January 1902, Ida arrived at 26 East 57th
Street, Rogers' home, to find out.

Henry Rogers, tall, handsome, with a bushy white mous-
tache, greeted her at the door. He appeared to be about
sixty years old and had what Ida called "a trace of early
oil adventure in his bearing in spite of his air of authority,
his excellent grooming, his manner of the quick-witted
naturally adaptable man who has seen much of people."

"When and where did your interest in oil begin?"
Rogers asked.

Ida told him that she had grown up along Oil Creek,
near Rouseville, Pennsylvania, and therefore knew the oil
industry firsthand.

Rogers smiled. "Of course! Tarbell's Tank Shops! I
knew your father. I could put my finger on the spot
where those shops stood."

For a few minutes the two talked like old friends.
Rogers said that he and his family had lived close by,
in "a little white house with a high peaked roof."

"Oh, I remember it!" Ida couldn't conceal her surprise.
"The prettiest house in the world, I thought." She could
picture their houses on adjoining hills, separated by a
narrow ravine, a path at each side.

"Up that path I used to carry our washing every Monday morning and go for it every Saturday night," said Rogers. "Probably I've seen you hunting flowers on your side of the ravine. How beautiful it was! I was never happier."

Then the conversation turned serious. "What are you basing your story on?" Rogers asked.

"On documents," Ida told him.

"Why didn't you come to us at the start?"

"It wasn't necessary. You have written your history. Besides, it would have been quite useless," Ida answered, reminding Rogers that his company maintained a policy of secrecy.

"We've changed our policy. We are giving out information."

The more they talked, the more Ida liked this "robber baron." As she later related it,

We made a compact. I was to take up with him each case in their history. . . . He was to give me documents, figures, explanations, and justifications—anything and everything which would enlarge my understanding and judgment. I realized how big a contribution he would make if he continued to be as frank as he was in this preliminary talk. I made it quite clear to him, however, that while I should welcome anything in the way of information and explanation that he could give, it must be my judgment, not his, which prevailed.

In the meantime Ida's first article appeared in *McClure's.*

10

The Muckraker

Ida continued to meet with Henry Rogers for discussions that were always pleasant and completely frank.

"I could not shock Mr. Rogers with records," said Ida later, "even when I confronted him one day with the testimony he had given on a certain point which he admitted was not according to the facts. He curtly dismissed the subject, saying 'They had no business prying into my private affairs.' As for rebates, he explained, 'Somebody would have taken them if we had not.'"

"But with your strength, Mr. Rogers, you could have forced fair play on the railroads and on your competition," Ida argued.

"Ah, but there was always somebody without scruples in competition, however small that somebody might be. He might grow," added Rogers.

At the conclusion of the interview Rogers asked Ida if she would be willing to talk with John D. Rockefeller.

"Certainly," she answered.

"I'll try to arrange it," he said, shaking her hand warmly.

Back at her desk Ida scanned the evidence spread out in front of her—evidence of railroad rebates, patent infringements, "planned blackmail," and just plain bad faith. Ida could not accept Rogers' justifications.

Years before, she had listened sympathetically, but with some reservation, to independent oilmen who charged that the railroads were giving Standard Oil information about the size and destination of their shipments. Standard Oil, they claimed, encouraged the railroads to sidetrack tank cars carrying the independent refiner's petroleum and pressured his customers into canceling orders and buying from them instead.

Ida had never quite believed it. Now, unexpectedly, she had new—and conclusive—evidence. It seemed that a sixteen-year-old office boy who worked in a Standard Oil plant was burning discarded papers when he recognized the name of an independent oil refiner who had been his Sunday School teacher. Looking closely, he found that the man's name appeared on many bookkeeping sheets and in several letters. His curiosity aroused, he read the top sheet and discovered that Standard Oil was receiving full information from railroad offices concerning the refiner's oil shipments. Here, too, were copies of letters from the local Standard Oil office written to their representatives in the area to which the oil was being shipped. "Stop that shipment—get that trade," said one letter. Another spelled out exactly how this should be done.

Scooping up the records and letters, the boy took them to the refiner who, as it turned out, had read Ida's article. He promptly took the incriminating material to her.

With this evidence in hand, Ida went once again to call on Henry Rogers. This time she asked him, "Do you follow independent shipments? Do you stop them? Do you have the help of railroad shipping clerks in the operation?"

Once again he told her, "Of course, we do everything we can that is legal and fair to find out what our competitors are doing, just as you do in *McClure's Magazine*. But, as for any system of tracking and stopping, as you suggest, that is nonsense."

Without showing Rogers the material in her possession, she left. He would read it later in *McClure's*.

Now, as she thought about Rogers and what he had said, she wrote:

Very often people who admit the facts, who are willing to see that Mr. Rockefeller has employed force and fraud to secure his ends, justify him by declaring, "It's business." That is, "it's business" has come to be a legitimate excuse for hard dealing, sly tricks, special privileges. It is a common enough thing to hear men arguing that the ordinary laws of morality do not apply in business. Now, if the Standard Oil Company were the only concern in the country guilty of the practices which have given it monopolistic power, this story never would have been written. Were it alone in these methods, public scorn would long ago have made short work of the Standard Oil Company. But it is simply the most conspicuous type of what can be done by these practices. The methods it employs with such acumen, persistence, and secrecy are employed by all sorts of business men, from corner grocers up to bankers. . . .

And what are we going to do about it? [Ida asked her readers.] For it is our business. We, the people of the United States, and nobody else, must cure whatever is wrong in the industrial situation, typified by this narrative of the growth of the Standard Oil Company. That our first task is to secure free and equal transportation privileges by rail, pipe and waterway is evident. It is not an easy matter. It is one which may require operations which will seem severe; but the whole system of discrimination has been nothing but violence, and those who have profited by it cannot complain if the curing of the evils they have wrought bring hardship in turn on them. At all events, until the transportation matter is settled, and settled right, the monopolistic trust will be with us, a leech in our pockets, a barrier to our free efforts.

It was November 1902. Ida had spent three years hunting for the facts, traveling, interviewing, writing. Now that work began to pay off in a series of articles that rocketed *McClure's* to first place among the crusading magazines and made Ida Tarbell a name to be reckoned with.

11

The "Joan of Arc" of the Oil Industry

With each installment Ida probed deeper, exposing the smallest details of Standard Oil operations to public scrutiny. Still she met regularly with Henry Rogers—until several months into 1903, when the office boy's evidence appeared in print.

That day Henry Rogers was not smiling. "Where did you get that stuff?" he asked, pointing to the most recent issue of *McClure's*. His face was white with rage.

"Mr. Rogers," Ida answered quietly, "you can't for a moment think I would tell you where I got it. . . ."

After several curt exchanges on other points, both realized their discussion served no purpose. Ida made no more appointments. Nor was there any further possibility of an interview with John D. Rockefeller.

Only once in her lifetime did Ida ever see Rockefeller in person. The occasion was a Sunday School meeting at the Cleveland church he attended. Rockefeller, who spent his summers in Cleveland and his winters in New York, was concluding his summer visit and using the meeting to say good-bye to his church friends.

A friend of Ida, hearing that Rockefeller would speak

that evening, urged her to come. "You must at least look at Mr. Rockefeller," he said.

Despite her guilt feelings at seeing a man who didn't want to see her, Ida went to the meeting. Entering the Sunday School room along with church members, she hoped Rockefeller would never learn of her presence there. For Ida, this was an experience she would remember vividly all her life. In her late seventies, she could still describe the dismal meeting room and John D. Rockefeller, an elderly but powerful figure speaking in a clear voice about what he called "the dividends of righteousness."

When the meeting was over, Ida moved with everyone else to the church sanctuary. There she watched him take his place in the family pew. Rockefeller seemed uneasy, turning his head constantly from side to side, searching the faces of his friends, as though trying to guess their thoughts.

Rockefeller's opinion of Ida was relayed to her secondhand by a mutual friend who had suggested to him that he reply to her articles. He reportedly answered, "Not a word. Not a word about that misguided woman."

To another who questioned him about Ida's charges, he said, "All without foundation. The idea of the Standard forcing anyone to sell his refinery is absurd. The refineries want to sell to us, and nobody that has sold or worked with us but had made money . . . [and was] glad he did so.

"I thought once of having an answer made to the *McClure* articles, but you know it has always been the policy of the Standard to keep silent under attack and let their acts speak for themselves."

As each of Ida's articles appeared—eighteen in all

—Americans the country over, from President Theodore Roosevelt himself to the farmers in rural Kansas, recognized the by-line of Ida M. Tarbell, "the lady muckraker." For her part, Ida did not enjoy the newfound fame. Behind the powerful pen of a muckraker hid a shy historian, and this was the person she preferred to be.

In 1904 the articles were collected and published, along with an appendix of documents, in two thick volumes.

Reviewers, editorial writers, satirists added their comments on her work. An unknown poet wrote the following poem:

The Lady With the Muck Rake

Maud Tarbell, on a Summer's day,
(Her name was Ida, by the way.

But we must call her Maud, or she
Could not be in this parody).

Maud Tarbell, so the tale befell,
(We think her name's pronounced Tar-belle)

But we must see the accent wrong,
Or else exclude her from this song.

Maud Tarbell (now our gait we've struck)
Raked in the oil fields, black with muck,

Raked high and low, and fore and aft,
And heaped up windows full of graft.

John D. leaned lankly o'er the fence,
Arrayed in jeans and innocence.

Quoth he: "This muck-strewn field forsake,
And lay aside that loathsome rake."

But Maud, with sure and steady aim,
Kept right on raking just the same.

Said John: "I hope you won't rake me;
My life is led in piety.

Don't rake around my humble cot."
But Maud serenely said: "That's what?"

And calmly raked a few more lines,
Until John was tangled in the tines.

John seldom swears, but after that
His friends o'erheard him mutter, "Drat!"

"Of all the words that bring bad luck,
The saddest are these: Folks *will* rake muck."

The most vociferous attack was an essay written by a man named Elbert Hubbard, an author and founder of the Roycroft Press in East Aurora, New York. Wrote Hubbard: "Ida Tarbell . . . is an honest, bitter, talented, prejudiced and disappointed woman who wrote from her own point of view. And that view is from the ditch where her father's wheelbarrow was landed by a Standard Oil tank-wagon. . . . She shot from cover, and she shot to kill. Such literary bushwackers should be answered shot for shot."

It was said that five million copies of this essay, printed in pamphlet form, were ordered by Standard Oil and distributed by Mr. Hubbard.

Among magazine reviewers, there were many different reactions: one praised her objectivity, another condemned her bias.

A writer for *Public Opinion*, a magazine supervised by Samuel McClure's brother Robert, wrote: "The author never gets excited, however exciting her story may become; she sets forth the facts, and to a considerable extent leaves inference and conclusions to her readers. . . . It is, in effect, a liberal education in the fundamentals of the trust problem. . . ."

Colliers' Weekly, a rival of *McClure's,* agreed, saying: "Never was a contemporaneous history so temperately and accurately written."

A harsher reaction came from *The Nation:* "This book seems to have been written for the purpose of intensifying the popular hatred. The writer has either a vague conception of the nature of proof, or she is willing to blacken the character of Mr. John D. Rockefeller by insinuation and distraction. . . ."

But in 1940, historian Allan Nevins, writing with the historical perspective of twenty-five years, declared that *The History of the Standard Oil Company* was "the greatest book produced by the muckraking movement . . . its most enduring achievement."

Whatever the opinions of reviewers, there could be no doubt of public reaction. Ida was the nation's number-one anti-Standard Oil spokesman. Her desk overflowed with letters applauding her work. Also, there were letters from individuals who had grievances against the company. Many had legitimate complaints and sought reasonable adjustments; others, revenge or personal notoriety.

One of those who contacted Ida was Frank Rockefeller, brother of John D., who sent word that he possessed incriminating documents worthy of publication. Surprised to hear from a member of the Rockefeller family and realizing the potential importance of such a story, Ida agreed to meet with him in Cleveland.

There she found a bitter man who accused his brother

of "robbing" him of Standard Oil stock. The truth was that Frank Rockefeller had borrowed money from his brother and offered his stock as collateral. When Frank was unable to repay the loan, John took the stock instead. From John's point of view, his action was morally justified because he believed his brother was too frivolous and spent money too freely. Frank Rockefeller's complaint was not against the Standard Oil Company but against the brother who had cut him out of the profits.

In this matter Ida could not fault John D. Rockefeller. He was completely within his legal rights, and that was all that concerned her. She was horrified that brother should turn against brother, but this was a family matter, and she wanted no part of it.

As the public outcry against Standard Oil grew louder, would-be reformers stood before large audiences and called attention to John D. Rockefeller's large donations to colleges and churches. "Do not touch tainted money," they thundered, warning against donations "done to silence criticism."

Ida was appalled. She knew that Rockefeller had always contributed a generous portion of his earnings to philanthropies, and she felt that such attacks were unjustified. Her own writing had been objective, impersonal, and backed up by documents every inch of the way.

But there was no escape from the mass emotions stirred up by *The History of the Standard Oil Company*. She was disappointed in the reaction of the public. "I had hoped the book might be received as a legitimate historical study," she said, "but to my chagrin I found myself included in a new school, that of the muckrakers."

Unwillingly drawn into the fierce aftermath of an exposé, Ida wished she could shake loose of her subject and, as she had always done in the past, escape to another. This time, however, author and subject were too closely identified. The currents of the time caught her up and carried her along.

The American oil industry now shifted its major operations from Pennsylvania to Kansas and Oklahoma. Not far behind went Ida Tarbell.

The Standard Oil "methods" which she had reported in such detail were being "adapted" to the new oil rush sweeping through Kansas and into Oklahoma in 1907. As word spread of rich oil strikes and flowing wells, Standard Oil moved in, accumulating leases, establishing drilling operations, and laying pipelines. Once again the trust was forcing independent oilmen out of business.

This time, however, the independents took immediate action, as citizens of Kansas demanded that the state enact protective regulations. Several legislators responded by introducing bills that would control rates for both railroad shipping and oil pipelines. Another, pointing out that Kansas owned a hemp factory that operated within the state penitentiary, suggested that the penitentiary run a state-owned oil refinery. The governor spoke out in favor of the plan. The legislature agreed.

From Kansas, Ida hired a buckboard drawn by two horses and rode south into the Indian territory of Oklahoma. Word of her visit spread rapidly, and independent oilmen greeted her as their heroine.

Ida, collecting information for further articles, only wanted to be left alone, but nevertheless she found herself "dragged to the front as an apostle," as she later described it.

Arriving late one night in the newly established town of Tulsa, Oklahoma, she checked into the best accommodations available—"a rough little hostelry where I was so suspicious of the look of things that I moved the bureau against the lockless door."

The next morning the local newspaper editor invited her to his office for breakfast and conversation. No sooner had they entered than a forty-piece band, trombones and trumpets blaring, appeared at the window. Three of the bandsmen were Indians in full tribal regalia. Marching behind the band was the predominantly male population of Tulsa.

The men, knocking on the doors and windows of the office, hollered "Speech! Speech!" Not knowing what to say to such a group, Ida handed the office boy several dollar bills. "Quick," she said. "Go buy cigars, enough for everyone out there!"

Instead of speaking, she moved among the men, smiling and handing out cigars. No one cared that she didn't speak. Many wouldn't have understood her if she had. She heard one Indian, obviously pleased with the cigar, tell his friends, "He all right!"

That afternoon Ida rode with local dignitaries in a parade through the city. As honored guest, she rode in a barouche, a horse-drawn carriage with an elevated driver's seat at the front.

The next day, her arms filled with candy, flowers, and other gifts from the people of Tulsa, Ida was on her way back to Kansas to get the rest of her story. First stop: the office of Governor Hoch.

The governor was opening his mail when Ida walked in. He showed her many letters praising the plan for state control of oil refining. Some letter writers had even urged him to become a candidate for the presidency of the United States.

Although the governor supported public ownership, he was quick to point out that he was not a socialist. He believed in the competitive system and "was not trying to force private industry out of the state." He merely wanted private industry to be reasonable—the private industry being, of course, the Standard Oil Company.

Jubilant Kansans who supported the new legislation scheduled victory celebrations across the state. They invited Ida to speak before the largest gathering. She agreed, but to the disappointment of those who hoped to hear a heated attack on Standard Oil, the "Joan of Arc of the oil industry," as one man called her, spoke instead of the independent oilman's responsibilities.

"Your problem now is to do business," she told them. "As far as laws can insure it you have free opportunity; but good laws and free opportunity alone do not build up a business. Unless you can be as efficient and as patient, as farseeing as your great competitor—laws or no laws, you will not succeed. You must make yourselves as good refiners, as good transporters, as good marketers, as ingenious, as informed, as imaginative in your legitimate undertakings as they are in both their legitimate and illegitimate."

Other oil-producing states now followed Kansas in enacting laws that would protect their citizens from being overwhelmed by the monopoly. In Washington, President Theodore Roosevelt proved to be a good deal less friendly to big business than his predecessor, William McKinley, had been. Beginning with a trust-busting campaign, Roosevelt now responded to popular demand by asking Congress to pass legislation establishing a Department of Commerce and Labor, which would have the power to investigate corporations, examine their books, and even question their employees. "If you do not pass it this session," he told Congress, "I will call an extra session."

Of course, Standard Oil and the nation's other trusts opposed such legislation and fought back by bringing political pressure against its supporters. Fearful of the trusts' strength, President Roosevelt issued a statement quoting a telegram allegedly sent by John D. Rockefeller to members of the United States Senate: "We are opposed to any antitrust legislation—it must be stopped." To this day no one knows if such a telegram actually existed, but the President's statement caused new public outcries. Congress immediately passed the legislation.

As everyone expected, the first job assigned the new department by the President was an investigation of the nation's oil industry. In 1906, the investigators announced publicly that they had proof the Standard Oil Company had received preferential shipping rates from railroads. Shortly after this announcement, the United States government brought suit against the great company.

One day not long after that, Ida, waiting to cross New York's busy Fifth Avenue, saw Henry Rogers pass by in an open automobile. Seeing her, he smiled and waved.

Ida was surprised and pleased. Perhaps he harbored no ill will after all. She remembered their conversations and Rogers' disarming frankness. If he would only put down his recollections with that same frankness, she thought, what a historical document he could produce!

That same day Ida requested an appointment, and just as quickly, Rogers agreed.

The two met cordially. Henry Rogers, as frank as ever, had suffered a stroke a short time before. He had returned to his office in time to cope with the action of the Federal government, but he was not well. With some bitterness, he spoke of trustbuster Theodore Roosevelt's interference with big business.

In a moment of reflection, he talked about the early days of the oil industry. "There is a whole chapter that has not been written, that from 1859 to 1872," he said. Rogers leaned back in his chair. The short conversation had tired him. "We'll talk about this again."

But there were no more meetings. Henry Rogers died suddenly in May of 1909. Two years later, the Supreme Court of the United States dissolved the Standard Oil Company.

12

The Unlikely Farmer

At fifty, Ida was famous, admired, and respected by millions of people who looked to her as spokesman for the public interest. In the eyes of many, she deserved special praise as "a woman who won her honors in competition with men."

"She must have *achieved* her distinction. It had not just dropped into her lap," said other women who understood the female struggle for recognition in the male-oriented business world.

There was truth in this, of course, but Ida dismissed such remarks as unfair to her male colleagues. Working with men, she insisted, had never been a handicap. In fact, because they treated her more politely and with greater respect than they did her male counterparts, she felt that being a woman was an advantage rather than a disadvantage.

Ida's strong accusations against Standard Oil made her writing sound strong as well, and to her amusement, she was often described as "a woman who thinks and acts like a man." Occasionally, someone meeting her for the first time blurted out his surprise: "You're not a bit like what I thought you were! I imagined you were short—and aggressive!"

That mental picture was wrong on both counts. Ida was taller than most women and many men. As for being aggressive, a friend, in a burst of poetic affection, described her quite differently: "She is no more aggressive than a tree, which grows by some quiet and natural process, and gives with the same quietness and naturalness . . . something that roots deep and that reaches high; something that suggests shelter and pleasantness and relief; but which at the same time suggests a continuing growth and abundant vitality. If you love trees, you will know what I mean."

Young ladies of the early 1900's who read newspaper accounts of Ida's meetings with the nation's leaders and who followed her opinions on important problems thought about their own future: "A woman *could* do things like that!"

Those who admired Ida from afar saw only her strengths. They would never believe that such a woman could be dissatisfied with her life. For Ida, however, being a public figure carried with it an overwhelming sense of obligation which demanded constant fulfillment. Although she recognized in herself the fierce discipline that had driven her to success in a field she had not chosen, she could not relax when there was work to be done.

For most of her life, Ida had been too busy to realize that some day, as a result of her self-imposed rigors, she would be overwhelmed by the simple human need for belonging, for a sense of permanence which work in itself could not offer. When she was traveling, sometimes for months at a time, she lived out of a suitcase, coming back at the end of the day to a rented room where she sat alone sorting her notes and packing for the next stop on her itinerary. Day after day, she interviewed strangers whose faces she would never see again.

Even when she finally returned to her tiny apartment in New York City, her routine varied little. At least in New York she had some friends, mostly staff people from *McClure's,* who invited her to dinner, or she invited them, or perhaps they would attend an occasional concert together.

But for a writer who works where she lives, as Ida did most of the time, even an occasional evening out may not be enough to refresh one's spirit or to change the pattern of weariness. In a small apartment like Ida's, the work was always there, beckoning accusingly when the writer returned.

For the first time, Ida saw herself as a lonely middle-aged woman whose entire life was her work. After years of assignments, completing one and beginning another, what had she to show for her efforts? Money, of course. Frugal living and careful management had brought security. She was not wealthy, but a regular salary from *McClure's* had allowed her to save the windfalls of her free-lance writing—payments for articles, advances on books in progress, and royalties when they were published.

But with maturity had come the realization that neither work, economic security, nor even fame were enough for happiness. What she needed was a home. Titusville —and her family—were five hundred miles from New York, too far for a weekend visit. For them to visit her for any length of time was impossible; her apartment was too small.

New York itself was growing bigger, and so was Ida's

list of daily irritations: the increasing city noises, the heavier traffic, the people who stared straight ahead and never smiled. She needed a place of escape, a home of her own where she could enjoy complete quiet.

One weekend in 1906, while driving with friends through the unpaved back roads of Connecticut, she saw a "For Sale" sign in front of an abandoned farmhouse. The house, shielded by two huge oaks and a row of pines, stood at the top of a small hill. It was surrounded by fifty acres of land, thick with underbrush and weeds. The apple trees, neglected for years, needed trimming and spraying. The roof leaked, and there was no indoor plumbing. To Ida, the farm seemed like a child asking to be adopted.

Easton Corners, as the tiny farm community was called, was only eight miles from Bridgeport, a short train ride from New York City. The New York apartment would be her "workshop"; the Easton Corners farm, her home.

At first her new neighbors, awed by the presence of a celebrity in their community, watched for glimpses of the great lady. What they saw was "a placid, smiling housewife" and not, as they expected, "the wielder of the trenchant pen." Sometimes they saw her feeding her newly acquired dogs, all four of them yipping at her heels. Other times, they saw her hanging clothes on the line behind the house.

Years later a nearby farmer admitted the skepticism they had all felt earlier: "Why, when she first came here we were scary about having so smart a person for a neighbor, but she ain't that way at all. She's just the same as us folks."

Nevertheless, their familiarity was tempered with respectful affection. They called her "our Miss Tarbell."

In her own eyes, whenever Ida was living at the farm she was "first a farmer and incidentally, a writer." Here she could relax. After the deaths of her mother and father, her sister Sara, who had never married, moved there, too. Their brother Will and his wife visited for long periods of time.

The farmhouse was attractive, with bright patterned rugs partially covering well-waxed wood plank floors. The furniture was sturdy and comfortable. In every room, including the hallway, there was at least one bowl or vase, usually filled with flowers which Ida picked and arranged herself. Her pewter collection—candlesticks, plates, bowls, and tankards, gathered piece by piece over the years—lined the mantel above the fireplace in the dining room. But on the whole Ida was more concerned with comfort and utility than with making the house into a showplace.

Ida's newfound happiness was predictable. Her childhood fascination with biology, displaced in the course of life's realities, had finally been satisfied. As a farmer, she was now the scientist she had once intended to be. "Most interesting," she said, "are the limitless experiments which may be made in a garden."

Once she contacted the United States Department of Agriculture in Washington, "a veritable god-mother to the farmer," and arranged to take part in one of their projects. Her description of this is more enthusiastic than anything she ever said about her writing: "I am nursing trees which the Bureau of Plant Industry has gathered in many countries for the purpose of acclimation," she explained. "To see what will happen in Connecticut to a willow from Chile or to a cherry from Japan is good fun!"

After a few years the farm was self-sustaining. "My

garden, my fruit trees, my cow and my poultry yard feed me and whatever guests I may have," she said. "In winter I can heat my little house with wood cut from my place, and live abundantly from the well-stocked vegetable cellar and fruit closet."

Ida's casual remarks made farm life sound simple. Perhaps it was, in contrast to her city work. But behind her easygoing manner was the canny mind of a shrewd businesswoman who spent long hours weighing alternatives and making careful decisions. Well aware of her costs and profits, she told a friend, "Seeds are the most profitable investment I know about. A five-cent package of lettuce seed brings in a return of about two thousand percent on the money invested."

Obviously she managed the farm with the same thoroughness she put into her writing.

Her writing, however, remained her first duty. She set aside an upstairs room as a "library" and went there to work each morning after breakfast.

It was a room with three large windows and bright with morning sunlight. In the best light stood an unpolished mahogany desk piled high with papers and mail-order catalogs. On three sides of the room were low bookshelves filled with books on Ida's favorite subjects—peace, suffrage, gardening, birds, and livestock. One shelf had only books of fiction. A stone fireplace, laid with logs and tinder, was ready for lighting on the first cool day of fall.

Friends from the city who dropped in for a visit often found her puttering in the kitchen. She never considered herself much of a cook, but once a year, usually in the fall, she invited fifty or sixty of her nearest neighbors for a special dinner which she cooked herself. At least on one occasion the menu required some skill. There was suckling pig, roasted with an apple in its mouth, baked potatoes and squash from the garden, fresh cider, and pumpkin pie.

Another time a magazine interviewer arrived to find Ida stirring a boiling kettle of jelly.

"My friends refuse to take me seriously as a farmer," said Ida to the woman, "but at Christmastime this jelly shall prove to them that I am most practical and worthy of my farm. Provided," she added, "the ants don't get it first."

Although Ida could usually arrange to spend weekends and summers at the farm, she was obliged to stay for long periods of time at her New York apartment in order to gather research materials and confer with editors. "Frankly," she said, "I return to the city to make money to support my farm. Someday I hope that the plan on which I am working will bring me to the point where I shall feel justified in breaking with the town altogether and retiring to the comforting and quieting companionship of the real country; but I'm afraid that is a long way off."

She was right. In the same year she bought her farm, Ida also broke with *McClure's*. McClure had become interested in some highly speculative ventures, which, in the opinion of stockholders, some of whom were also staff members, jeopardized the publishing company's future. By this time, Ida had a twenty-thousand-dollar interest in the company, and she and the other staff members were worried about their investments. After several emotional scenes, with McClure and Ida both weeping because they were unable to agree on the company's future direction, she and the others asked McClure either to buy or sell. McClure decided to keep the company. Ida and her colleagues pooled their assets and bought a long-established magazine, *The American,* formerly known as *Frank Leslie's Illustrated Monthly.* In October of 1906, the group's first issue of *The American* was published. Ida's assignment—a history of the tariff from the Civil War on—took her back to Washington.

13

All in the Day's Work

Through the final years of the nineteenth century and well into the twentieth, the tariff was as important an issue as the monopolies. Powerful men with business interests in commodities such as wool, cotton, iron, or sugar wanted to keep out foreign goods which were low priced and therefore competitive with their own. These men favored a high protective tariff that taxed imports. They formed "lobby" groups, so called because they waited in the lobbies of the Capitol where they could talk to—and influence—the nation's lawmakers. Often, they sweetened their arguments with bribery or, that failing, threatened political ruin for legislators who opposed them.

Once again Ida was indignant. These men, interested only in their personal profits, had no regard for the American public which, as a result of the existing tariff, was forced to pay higher prices.

Ready to take up her pen once again, Ida went to Princeton, New Jersey, where Grover Cleveland lived in retirement. The former President shared her concerns but pointed out that he had been helpless during both of his terms in office. Despite his tariff message of 1887, he explained, the Congress had failed to revise the schedules.

From Princeton she went to Washington where she searched through old Congressional Records and tariff documents. Her notebooks crammed full of information, Ida returned to the farm. She was certain that when the American public understood the issue, they would demand action from the men they had elected to Congress.

Her first manuscript completed, she sent a copy to former President Cleveland for his comments. A few weeks later, he wrote back: "Your article has caused me to feel again the greatest sorrow and disappointment I have ever suffered in my public career—the failure of my party to discharge its most important duty and its fatuous departure from its appointed mission."

Further, said President Cleveland, the tariff was "a vicious, inequitable, illogical tax."

Though Congress had failed to act, public opinion was mounting. In the next presidential election, William Howard Taft ran on a platform that called "unequivocally" for tariff reform. Soon after his inauguration, he requested his aides to begin work toward that goal.

Tariff-protected manufacturers protested, pointing out that a high tariff would enable them to pay higher wages to their workers. What they didn't say, however, was that only 2.5 million workers out of the 17.5 million in the nation's work force were employed in tariff-protected industries. Thus, 15.5 million American workers whose wages would not be increased would be subjected to higher prices. These consumers were apparently unimportant.

This point had been made clear during congressional

hearings which preceded the tariff vote. Lawyer Louis Brandeis, who was later to become a Supreme Court Justice, prepared to testify:

"For whom do you appear?" the committee chairman asked.

"For the consumer," answered lawyer Brandeis.

The committee laughed uproariously at the thought of anyone representing the consumer.

Perhaps it was simply a question of understanding, thought Ida. Only recently Jane Addams, the noted social worker, had told her that before reading her latest article, she "never knew what the tariff meant. . . ." Now she was convinced that it increased the cost of life's basic necessities, thus seriously affecting the poor.

Working at the mahogany desk in the farm "library," Ida wrote:

"As far as the tariff is concerned, public opinion has never been fairly embodied in the bills adopted. If the popular understanding of protection as expressed in our elections had been conscientiously followed, there would be no duties on iron and steel products, on cheap cottons and cotton mixtures, and certainly none on a great variety of raw materials probably including raw wool."

After the publication of this article, a group of progressive senators expressed their concern. Ida met with one of them, Senator Dolliver of Iowa. "I have been going on for twenty years," said the senator, "taking practically without question what they handed me; but these alliances between the party and industrial interests have set me to thinking. I begin to understand something of the injustice being done the consumer."

Nevertheless, despite increasing interest on the part of insurgents like Dolliver, the law that Congress finally passed was, in Ida's words, "without principles or morals." Even President Taft, who signed the measure into law, admitted that it was politically necessary and tailored to the demands of the lobbyists. Fairness to the consumer, apparently, was never an issue.

Convinced that there would never be a fair tariff "as long as tariffs were set by a Congress under the thumb of people personally interested," Ida now turned her attention to another phase of American industry—the progress of the factory worker.

For years, muckrakers had brought the plight of the factory worker to national attention, creating a familiar picture in their writings: dangerous working conditions, poorly ventilated buildings, lack of sanitation facilities, bad housing conditions, and undernourished children.

Some Americans believed that such problems were inherent in the capitalistic system and that only the destruction of the system itself would solve them. Others, like Ida, believed that progress could be made within the existing system, in fact, was already being made. Ida intended to tell the American public what was being done.

In 1912, *American Magazine* commissioned Ida to write a series of articles on this subject. For the next four years she zigzagged through the United States, visiting industrial towns. She went from Pittsburgh's steel mills to the coal mines of West Virginia, from the candy factories in Philadelphia to the breweries and tanneries of Wisconsin, from New England shoe factories to New York City's garment industry.

In all, she visited fifty-five major companies, interrupting her tour only briefly for short vacations at the farm in Connecticut.

"My first move in a factory was to study the processes

of the particular industry," she explained. "Machines were not devils to me as they were to some of my reforming friends. To me machines freed from heavy labor, created abundance . . . I was able to understand what the enemy of the machine rarely admits: that men and women who have arrived at the dignity of steady workers not only respect, but frequently take pride in their machines."

She interviewed hundreds of workers, spending as much time in their homes as she did in the factories. Wherever she went, even into the plainest of company-owned row houses, she found women whose housekeeping skills made their homes attractive. One man, obviously proud of his home, led her from room to room as he pointed out the potted geraniums on the living room table, the hand-embroidered curtains at the bedroom windows, "his Sunday clothes . . . hung on hangers with a calico curtain in front to keep them clean."

Often routine patterns of everyday life overlaid deep suspicions between company officials and workmen, and both groups, in time of disagreement, resorted to violence to settle their problems. Organized efforts to settle labor-management disputes by negotiation were still in the future.

On a day-to-day basis, however, supervisors and workers were friendly toward each other. Often, the company foreman lived around the corner from his father or brother who still worked in the mill or mine. Most likely, the company's "big boss" called the head of the labor union by his first name. Outwardly, there was polite respect; inwardly, there was antagonism, a feeling that the other was taking unfair advantage.

The more Ida saw, the more she was convinced that

industrial peace was possible only when an employer recognized workers' grievances and showed good faith in dealing with them.

One employer who left a lasting impression on her was Thomas Lynch, a former miner who worked his way from job to job until, halfway through life, he headed several large mines. This man, the originator of the famous slogan "Safety First," believed the welfare of the workmen was more important than his extra profits.

At the end of each day, Ida sat down before her new dictaphone and recorded her observations. With the series almost complete, she was growing restless and wanted to go back to her farm. Now sixty years old, she no longer wanted to be tied to a magazine staff position.

Then, too, the *American* had been sold in 1915 to the Crowell Publishing Company, which planned to change it into "a different type of magazine," and Ida felt that "there was no place for my type of work on the new *American*. If I were to be free I must again give up security."

Although she still hoped to write on any subject that captured her interest, for the time being she needed a change—perhaps even a change in profession.

President Wilson asked Ida in 1916 to serve as a member of his Tariff Commission. Despite her pleasure in being selected for such an honor, she had declined. "I had had no experience in the kind of work this required," she explained. "I was an observer and reporter, not a negotiator. I was not a good fighter in a group; I forget my duty in watching the contestants."

Jane Addams, outspoken in the struggle for women's rights, pleaded with Ida to accept "for the sake of women," but Ida told her, "Women, like men, serve in proportion to their fitness for office, to the actual fact they have something to contribute." The appointment on the Tariff Commission paid a large salary and carried great prestige. Yet Ida Tarbell felt she could best serve the cause of women by continuing to do what she did best—observing and reporting.

14

The Seventh Decade

Earlier, when the well-known Coit Alber Lecture Bureau had offered to send Ida through the country as a lecturer on American industry, she had scoffed at the idea. Now, in 1916, it looked like the change she was seeking. On impulse, she signed the contract.

Then, she had second thoughts. She had never even made a professional speech. The era of microphones was some years away, and any lecturer worth her salt was expected to have a strong voice.

Ida's diction, at least in everyday conversation, was good, but her voice was thin, lacking in resonance, and too weak to reach the people in the back rows.

Without delay, Ida hired a speech teacher from the American Academy of Dramatic Arts, and under his guidance, began a round of exercises. To strengthen her diaphragm, she lay flat on the floor with a pile of heavy books on her midsection. With each deep breath, the books moved up and down. This she did each morning and evening.

During the day as she moved around the house, she practiced lip movements and sounds—to increase resonance and projection: "ma, me, mi, mo, ba, be, bi, bo . . ." A few months later, when she joined the lecture tour, she knew, at least theoretically, how to make people hear her. She never developed a full, resonant voice, but according to at least one listener her speech was "natural and pleasing."

Although those who heard her agreed that she was "poised and sure," Ida herself felt otherwise. She never spoke without a glass of water within reach. If her attention was distracted for a moment, she could always pick up the glass, pretend to drink, gain time, and regain poise.

Life on the lecture circuit was somewhat like a circus —advance publicity and ticket sales, a brief stay in each town, and a performance in a tent. Of course, there were obvious differences, too. A lecture tour was more formal, and the audience was better dressed and more polite and serious minded.

At each town the tour director hired local boys to erect the red-trimmed khaki canvas they carried along. After securing the tent to the ground, they placed the sectioned wood flooring and swept the place scrupulously clean. They hung strings of electric light bulbs along the entrance and across the inside of the tent. At the front, they placed a small raised platform for the speaker and then neatly arranged rows of straight-back chairs.

The audience always arrived promptly and listened attentively. However, despite the applause and provocative questions which inevitably followed Ida's talk, it was obvious that interest in her subject was waning. With the nation worrying about war, domestic problems seemed less important. Even Ida herself lost interest in her subject as she read each day's headlines.

For more than a decade preceding 1914, Americans had watched the nations of Europe draw closer to war. However, the United States, safely separated from Europe by the Atlantic Ocean, had little interest in the economic rivalries, balance-of-power politics, and nationalistic policies propelling them toward a confrontation. When the actual fighting began in the summer of 1914, the United States immediately proclaimed neutrality. Now, however, it was becoming more difficult to remain neutral.

America watched the Germans blockade the waters around the British Isles and heard the pronouncement that its U-boats would sink Allied vessels without warning. On May 7, 1915, the Germans sank the Cunard Line's luxury liner, the *Lusitania,* and 128 Americans lost their lives.

Despite increased demands that the United States enter the war, President Wilson felt it wrong, asking that Americans remain "impartial in thought as well as deed."

"There is such a thing as a nation being so right that it does not need to convince others by force that it is right," said the President.

Several months later, two Americans were killed in the attack on the British passenger ship *Arabic.* As a result, the President threatened to break off diplomatic relations with Germany, but after the German ambassador assured him that German U-boats would no longer attack ships without warning, and in any case would certainly remove nonmilitary passengers to safety, he took no action.

In the 1916 presidential race American voters reelected peace candidate Wilson over his hawkish opponent, Charles Evans Hughes. Soon after the inauguration, Ida talked with the President at a dinner party given by Secretary of the Navy Josephus Daniels and his wife.

He told her, "I never go to bed without realizing that I may be called up by news that will mean that we are at war. It is harder because the reports that come to us must be kept secret. Hasty action, indiscretion might plunge us into a dangerous situation when a little care would entirely change the face of things. My great duty is not to see red."

Shortly after that, what Wilson feared most finally happened. German U-boats began their attacks once again. In March 1917, they sank three unarmed American merchant ships.

On April 2, 1917, President Wilson went to Congress with his war message:

"We must put excited feelings away. Our motive will not be revenge or the victorious assertion of the physical might of the nation, but only the vindication of right, of human right, of which we are only a single champion. . . .

"There is only one choice we cannot make, we are incapable of making—we will not choose the path of submission and suffer the most sacred rights of our nation and our people to be ignored or violated. The wrongs against which we now array ourselves are no common wrongs; they cut to the very root of human life. . . ."

Ida listened to these words, which took the nation into World War I, and wept.

A few weeks later, as she spoke before a dinner meeting in Cleveland, a Western Union messenger handed her a telegram from the President of the United States, asking if she would accept appointment to the Women's Committee of the Council of National Defense. Immediately, she wired back "Yes."

She canceled two book contracts and moved once again to the nation's capital.

The Women's Committee, like many other "anxious, confused, scrambling" groups had only a general understanding of its purpose. During the first meeting, the chairman explained that President Wilson had designated them as the official agency for coordinating the defense activities of the nation's women. The exact program they would work out together.

As each woman identified herself, Ida realized that she was the only woman in the room who was not president of a national women's organization. Among the groups represented was the National Suffrage Society, the Women's Federation of Clubs, the National Women's Council, the Colonial Dames, and the National League for Women's Service.

But before tackling the nation's problems, the committee had a problem of its own to solve. With new appointees flooding Washington, office space was at a premium. Patriotic Washingtonians offered their houses and apartments but most of these were located in residential areas, far from the offices of the permanent government agencies. A week after its first meeting, the committee was established officially in a dreary room on busy Pennsylvania Avenue. It had only a single table, and there were fewer chairs than members. Ida borrowed chairs from an adjoining office, and the women got down to business.

Within a few months, the committee had established branches in every state, county, and almost every community in the United States.

Their first consideration was the nation's food supply. Already there were shortages as men left the farms and went off to war. In answer to the need, local branches of the Women's Committee, following directives and detailed instructions sent from the office on Pennsylvania Avenue, planted gardens, canned vegetables and fruits, and relearned their grandmothers' methods of drying apples and corn.

The committee encouraged women to replace men who left their jobs in industry. As women moved to fill the vacancies, representatives of women's rights groups met in Kansas City to insist that industries receiving war contracts conform to government-established labor standards. "If women are to work," they said, "they must be protected."

Working closely with the Children's Bureau, the committee guided local groups in setting up supervised playgrounds and nursing centers where young children could be cared for while their mothers worked. The committee's bulletin carried news items describing "what women were doing in industry not only in this country but in others."

Without intending it, the Women's Committee had become a catalyst in the women's rights movement.

The committee's aim, as Ida saw it, was "to make our vast horde conscious of the needs of sisters at the machine, eager to support what the government had decided was right and just for her protection. . . . We did our part in proving that even in war determined women can not only prevent backward movements but even move ahead."

In November 1918, almost a year and a half after American entry into the war, an armistice brought the fighting to an end. Europe, at war for four years, had suffered dreadfully: 37 million men were dead, wounded, or missing; property worth hundreds of billions of dollars lay ruined. As the committee filed its final report, Ida's thoughts turned to her old friends in France, where much of the war had been fought. France needed help —food, clothing, medical supplies. Already American rehabilitation forces were being readied, and Ida wanted to go along.

"Are you interested in a series of articles on rehabilitation?" she asked the editor of *Red Cross Magazine*.

"Go ahead," said the editor.

In January 1919, Ida put on her new Red Cross uniform, packed high boots, blankets, sweaters, and woolen tights in one suitcase, chocolate bonbons and hams in another, and boarded a ship bound for France.

Paris, exciting Paris, was somber. The streets were filled with American troops—the "doughboys"—buying souvenirs while awaiting passage home. Seeing Ida in uniform, several asked her to help them select special gifts for loved ones.

In her first free moment, she headed for the Latin Quarter and her old neighborhood. At the entrance, where cheerful Madame Bonnet had once greeted her boarders the steps lay crumbled, the door boarded up. Below was a jagged gap filled with debris, where Ida's old landlady had been killed by a bomb explosion.

Farther along, past Saint Michel and Saint Germain, she could find no trace of the tiny *laiterie* where the "Countess" had come each day for a cup of coffee.

"Nothing has been mended in Paris for three years," a friend explained, "nothing painted, nothing replaced."

Madame Marillier was alive and well, though a bit thin. Handing Ida a list of war dead, she said, "Look, those are our dead. Read them. You will remember some of the names." Ida recognized the names of several young men who had attended Madame Marillier's Wednesday evening discussions.

Throughout France, food was scarce and expensive. An egg cost sixteen cents. Butter ranged in price from two to four dollars a pound. A small jar of honey cost a dollar and a half.

The Louvre and most of the small art galleries were still closed. When the German invasion seemed imminent, the French had shipped their national art treasures— paintings, sculpture, *belles choses*—to safe hiding places. Now, one small section of the Louvre was reopening. Ida, who was invited to the ceremonies, later described what she saw:

"Everybody was in black and went about with unsmiling but touching appreciation, hardly believing, it seemed to me, that again he or she was free to rejoice in beauty. It was like coming home after the funeral of a beloved member of a family."

The next stop on Ida's itinerary was Lens, formerly a major manufacturing and mining center. As far as one could see, the city was a mass of red brick fragments. Hardly a wall remained standing.

She found some people living in the remnants of basements; others, in abandoned enemy trenches. A Catholic nun, shepherding orphaned children into a makeshift shelter, told Ida that some of the youngest children remembered no other life. "They don't even know the civilized ways," she said. "You have no idea how difficult it is to teach them to use handkerchiefs."

Along the Belgian border, abandoned tanks and artillery outlined the devastation. Even the familiar sounds of barking dogs and laughing children were gone. For miles, there was only silence.

By the time Ida returned to the capital, the Paris Peace Conference was already in session. The "Big Four" —Woodrow Wilson of the United States, Vittorio Orlando of Italy, David Lloyd George of Great Britain, and Georges Clemenceau of France, plus emissaries from twenty-seven other countries, all professing their desire for peace, sought a settlement that would satisfy all participants.

Such a settlement is rarely possible. Already there was disagreement about who should represent individual nations, and what agreement he should seek.

At the conference, no one was permitted in the visiting galleries, and news reporters were given very little information. As a result, people back home were suspicious that representatives were making secret agreements among themselves.

Ida tried as best she could to follow the progress of the talks, and once each month wrote a lengthy commentary for her American readers.

The nations that had suffered the most were bitter and demanded severe penalties, including concessions of territory from Germany. President Wilson, however, made clear that the United States was not punitive. Instead, he asked that the conference accept his Fourteen Points, a plan he believed would prevent future wars.

Among other suggestions, he proposed that all nations reduce the size of their military forces and open all international agreements to public scrutiny. He asked that trade barriers be removed and, most important, that every nation be guaranteed the right to govern itself. To bring all this about, he proposed "a general association of nations," a League of Nations which would safeguard each country's independence and maintain the peace.

One by one, Wilson's suggestions were rejected. Finally,

however, they accepted what he considered the most important point—the establishment of a League of Nations. Pleased with his progress, the President hurried home to ask congressional approval for American participation.

Instead of support, President Wilson found hostility from a Congress angry that they had not been consulted about the decision making at the peace table. Many legislators challenged the President's judgment in advocating a League of Nations which, they believed, would involve the United States in other countries' affairs.

Ida's final article from Paris described the conference agreement and praised the League of Nations as "the largest and soundest joint attempt the world has ever seen, to put an end to war." Then she went home to tell American audiences about the plan.

Meanwhile, France, still afraid of Germany, asked the United States and Great Britain if they would come to her aid should Germany attack again before the League was a reality. Ida added this issue to her talks, and supported a provisional guarantee of protection to France for a limited period of time.

She expressed this opinion one night just before the appearance of famed political orator William Jennings Bryan. It was no surprise to Ida that Mr. Bryan vigorously opposed additional American support of France. It was well known that Wilson had replaced Bryan as his secretary of state in 1915 because, as a pacifist, Bryan had opposed loans to either side in the conflict.

Appalled that Ida should express a conflicting opinion directly before his own talk, Mr. Bryan told her, "The audience came to hear me. It is important that they know my views."

Perhaps that was true, Ida told him. But, she asked, shouldn't an audience hear both sides of the argument?

A few weeks later there was nothing more for either of them to say. Congress declared that the United States would not join the League of Nations.

Now in her sixties, Ida took an inventory of her thinking and decided that she would limit her writing and speaking to those subjects she considered most worthwhile. First, she wanted to expose the methods of any unscrupulous minority which might exploit the honest, hardworking majority. Second, she wanted "to help spread knowledge of all the intelligent efforts within and without industry and government, to put an end to militancy, and replace it with actual understanding." Third, she wanted to write more about Abraham Lincoln, "who had best shown how to carry out a program of cooperation based on the consideration of others."

With these goals in mind, she divided most of her time between her New York apartment and Easton Corners. She accepted only brief assignments—an appointment to President Wilson's Industrial Conference, which brought labor, management, and representatives of the public together to discuss the future of American industry, and later, an appointment to President Harding's Unemployment Conference. During her seventh decade, Ida wrote the biographies of two well-known industrialists and four more books on Lincoln.

In 1926, just before her sixty-ninth birthday, restlessness overtook her once again, and she agreed to spend several months in Italy. A new kind of dictatorship called Fascism had sprung up under the rule of a man named Benito Mussolini, and Ida wanted a closer look.

As she packed her suitcase, she recalled her visit

with Woodrow Wilson four years earlier. The Wilsons, no longer in the White House, had invited her to "drink tea" at their residence on S street. She remembered her shock at finding Mr. Wilson "a very sick man," unable to rise from a sitting position. His mind, however, was "clear and strong." The words he spoke that day now flooded her consciousness: " . . . democracy is in danger from interior revolution, it must learn to preserve itself."

Perhaps, thought Ida, the political situation in Italy can teach us how. Uneasy about the future of the United States, she wanted to find out about "the process of manacling a free government," as Mussolini's Fascists had done.

The end of World War I had found Italy in turmoil, with a dozen political parties all vying for power. For several years there was violence, sometimes guerrilla warfare. The country was divided between the very rich and the very poor. Many Italians, dissatisfied with their lives, refused to work and showed their frustrations by destroying factories and looting stores. In the early 1920's Fascism began building up a nationwide organization which included a wide mixture of extremists—republicans and monarchists, idealists and reactionaries, who opposed the Socialists. There were constant clashes, many violent. The Fascists almost always had more money, more arms—and more ruthlessness. Italy's government was weak and the Fascists went unpunished. The fighting between the rivals continued.

In 1922 the Italian Cabinet resigned. Parliamentary leaders refused to form a new Cabinet because they felt Parliament was too divided for any agreement to come about. Eventually, in 1922, a general strike was called throughout Italy. Mussolini used this opportunity to show his strength as the supposed defender of law and order. He challenged the government to prove its power by breaking the strike within forty-eight hours—"after which Fascism will assume full freedom to supplant the state." Fascists followed up on this challenge by seizing control of major towns and restoring law and order.

Mussolini had done what the government could not do.

Since then, Americans had viewed the dictatorship with detached curiosity. They agreed, however, that Italy was no place to visit.

"Don't go!" warned friends.

"Speak only Italian, not French," said others.

"If they search you, be cooperative."

"Always use the Fascist salute!"

Even an undersecretary in the State Department warned of possible arrest.

What Ida found in Italy, however, was quite different from expectations. On her first day in Rome, she located a newsstand that sold both British and French newspapers. So far, no one had expected her to salute, and she had not been searched.

As to the dictator himself, she found that although Mussolini had bitter critics, he also had much support. The comment heard most frequently praised him in a rather qualified way: "We don't accept his methods; we don't believe in dictatorship; but it is better than anarchy."

At this time Mussolini had been in office only four years. He had established land-redemption programs, extended water power, and expanded farm production. His alliance with Adolf Hitler was far in the future, but in the meantime his police state was serving as a model to future—and more savage—dictatorships.

Ida traveled through the rural areas of Italy, where

she could see the effects of the new regime on the lives of the people. Wherever she looked, the farms and fields were filled with men, women, and children cutting wheat or alfalfa, harvesting rice, or sorting tobacco leaves. In small towns, old women and young girls worked side by side, embroidering designs on linen.

At the same time, it was an ominous quiet. These people avoided political discussions and volunteered little information in replying to Ida's questions. Seeing everyone busy, and apparently peaceful, Ida wondered if only a dictator could bring a country out of chaos. The thought troubled her. Must people have a strong leader to force them to live harmoniously? Must they lose their freedom to bring about order? she wondered.

Next, Ida requested an interview with the Fascist leader himself, and he agreed to see her.

Arriving earlier than her appointment, she sat in an anteroom and watched visitors come and go. Eventually, a secretary ushered her into a long room. There, behind a highly polished desk, sat Benito Mussolini. He rose from his chair and in perfect English apologized for making her wait.

"Please sit down," he said, motioning to one of the large chairs in front of his desk. Then, switching to French, the square-jawed dictator described Italy's housing problems. "Men and women must have better places to live," he said. "You cannot expect them to be good citizens in the hovels they are living in." He spoke passionately, pounding the desk for emphasis. His face reddened and his voice grew stern as he outlined his plans for improving Italian living conditions.

At the conclusion of the interview, he bent low and kissed Ida's hand. Personable and charming, but nevertheless a dictator, she thought. Already dissident groups sought to depose Mussolini. In the few weeks Ida had been in Italy, there had been three attempts on his life.

Ida believed "the day would come when he would overreach himself in a too magnificent attempt, an attempt beyond the forces of his country and so of himself, and he would finally go down as Napoleon went down."

Eventually, Mussolini's attempts at conquest, his alliance with Hitler, his role in World War II made her prophecy come true. In 1945, Mussolini died at the hands of Italian partisans, but Ida did not live to see it.

15

Busy, as Usual

The day before Ida's seventy-eighth birthday, the *New York Herald Tribune* carried a story headlined "IDA M. TARBELL, 'WORKING AWAY' AT 3 NEW BOOKS."

The year was 1935, and it was a different world. The country was in another depression—many said it was the worst one yet. Another Roosevelt was in the White House —Franklin Delano Roosevelt, a distant cousin of the trust-busting President who had been the muckrakers' sometime ally thirty-five years ago. Some said he would be an even bigger trustbuster than his cousin Theodore.

Outside Ida's window lay the pleasant green square of Gramercy Park, with its statue of actor Edwin Booth. It was a reminder of the past, for it was Booth's deranged brother who had killed Abraham Lincoln. Even now, in the New York of 1935, Ida remembered that day in Rouseville when an eight-year-old girl saw her father trudge slowly up the hill and heard her mother call fearfully, "What is it, Frank?"

There was much to remember after seventy-eight years of living.

But Ida had little time to dwell on memories. The

reporter who came to her "workshop" at 120 East Nineteenth Street found her busy writing rather than reminiscing. Nor was she particularly interested in being interviewed.

"I thought I'd just forget about birthdays for two years," she told him, "and then make a grand splurge when I'm eighty. Have all my friends around, you know. Besides there isn't much you want, anyway. Just say the old lady is working away, that she's finished one book and started another, that she's healthy and cheerful. That's all there is to it."

She had just completed a book called *The Nationalizing of Business, 1878–1898,* and was well along on her autobiography!

On her eightieth birthday, she was still too busy for the "grand splurge." Her schedule was the same as usual —two hours of dictation followed by whatever time was necessary to revise the copy in longhand. On this occasion, however, no amount of discipline could keep her at the desk. The telephone rang incessantly; well-wishers stopped by to shake her hand; delivery boys brought packages.

The small apartment was filled with bouquets and baskets of flowers. Letters and telegrams, including one from Mrs. Franklin Delano Roosevelt, poured in by the hundreds. "Every good wish and affectionate greetings on your birthday," said Mrs. Roosevelt's telegram.

Ida sat down immediately and replied:

Dear First Lady,
  I am deeply touched that you who literally spend your days and nights in doing good to others should take the time to send me birthday congratulations. But as near as

*I can make out, all your life you have naturally gone about
doing the kind thing. Someday, God willing, I am going
to set down what I think you mean in this tremendous
long and perplexing effort to make a genuinely cooperative democracy.*

That afternoon, *The New York Times* honored Ida as a
special guest at the National Book Fair. She spoke briefly,
attacking social reformers who advocated retirement at
age sixty-five: "I am convinced," she said, "that we
should continue producing so long as we produce economically. And the test of that is—are we able to do
something that people want, people we don't know? If
so, it is up to us to continue serving."

The well-known Pen and Brush, a group of 250 women
writers and artists, who had reelected Ida president for
twenty-eight consecutive years, had planned a gala cele-
bration to mark her eightieth birthday, but instead Ida
chose to have a quiet dinner with her old friend, S. S. Mc-
Clure, and several others. Disappointed at her refusal, the
group planned another tribute: They printed Ida M.
Tarbell Christmas cards carrying her photograph.

At a time when most people look back, Ida looked
ahead. She still planned to retire to Easton Corners, but
for now, she had classes to teach at Bucknell University in
Lewisburg, Pennsylvania, at the University of Arizona, or
at her alma mater, Allegheny College.

At Allegheny, she conducted classes three times each
week for would-be writers. No longer strong enough to
stand for an hour, as she had once done on the lecture
circuit, she sat at the head of a long table surrounded
by thirty students.

"I never longed to write," she told the students,

"never dreamed of it as a career." She described her fascination with history and biography as the cause of her "inadvertent adventure as a muckraker."

"There is no part of the work of writing a biography which interests me so much as the gathering of the materials," she told them. "It is like going on a voyage of discovery into a new country—or so it should be. One should start by wiping out of his mind all that he knows about the man, start as if you had never before heard of him. Everything then is fresh, new. Your mind, feeding on this fresh material, sees things in a new way. You are making the acquaintance of one who, if he is worth writing about, grows more interesting to you whatever he has done or has not done as the time goes on."

To students who asked her advice about becoming journalists, she said, "That's up to you. If you want to do it more than anything else, as you say, go to it. Certainly, you should learn shorthand—that is a tool in your business. You need to learn to express yourself on a typewriter, instead of by longhand.

"A very good place to begin in journalism is on a local paper. Get a job of any kind—learn how a newspaper is made—what is necessary in making a newspaper. It may be that you cannot get any more than sweeping out the office to begin with. That's all right. If you have your eyes open and your ears open, you will see how news is collected—how it is written up. You should be always keeping your wits at work finding things that, to you, are worthwhile to write about and then writing them."

To another student, she explained, "What you need to do is to observe the life around you, study it, think about it, and try to set down how it reacts on you. Build up your work from where you are. Read the best short stories, study the magazines and what they are interested in . . . and it means work, work, work. The writer has to learn his own lessons. Don't get any notion that there are any short cuts. Go at it with all your might, and don't be discouraged."

Ida wintered in Arizona in 1943. She taught at the university there, and in her extra hours was consulting editor of *Letter*, a magazine published in Tucson.

In December, she went back to the farm in Connecticut. After that, as Ida would say, here are the facts:

BRIDGEPORT, Conn., Jan 6—
Miss Ida Minerva Tarbell, noted biographer and dean of women authors in this country, who won fame for her exposé of the Standard Oil "trust," died at 7:28 o'clock this morning of pneumonia in Bridgeport Hospital. Her age was 86. . . .

—The New York Times

January 7, 1944

TITUSVILLE, Pa., May 11—

The body of Ida M. Tarbell, noted biographer and historian, who died at Bridgeport, Conn., on Jan. 6, was buried today in the family plot in Woodlawn Cemetery here. The dean of American women writers was buried beside her father, one of northwestern Pennsylvania's pioneer oilmen, her mother and other members of the family. . . .

—The New York Times

May 12, 1944

ADDENDUM

Quotations from Ida Tarbell's Writings

On society:

"I could blueprint a state of society which, on paper, would seem an ideal Utopia. But it probably would become a tiresome place to live."

On teachers:

"I had a succession of teachers . . . who won my respect and I know now how well they deserved it for their intelligence, their devotion, their wise handling of a young generation, on the whole as disquieting as the one we have now."

On work:

"I see no more promising path than each person sticking to the work which comes his way. The nature of the work, its seeming size and importance matter far less than its right relation to the place where he finds himself. If the need at the moment is digging a ditch or washing the dishes, that is the greatest thing in the world for the moment. The time, the place, the need, the relation are what decide the value of the act."

On culture in 1890:

"They [women] wanted this [culture] with as much intensity as their men folks probably wanted money, though I doubt if they could have explained the reason for their ambition as concisely. . . .

"The painful and discouraging feature of the case was the idea many . . . had of culture. They did not understand it to be ripeness and sureness of mind, it was not taste, discrimination, judgment; it was an acquisition—something which came with diplomas and degrees and only with them. . . ."

On culture in 1940:

"The theory that culture follows a diploma is less popular than it was . . . [It has been succeeded by another theory] that culture results from seeing—hearing—sampling everything new in ideas, in movements, in music, in the drama and literature. All over the country the exponents of this theory chase culture from morning until night. It is they who can be depended on to fill a theater at ten or eleven in the morning to listen to a lecture on peace or the cancer cure, or suffrage. . . . It is they who are the instant ally of any cause which is new and it is they who will stay by as long as the campaign is exciting —or until something more exciting looms in sight. . . ."

On the militant woman in the women's rights movement:

" . . . the militant woman frequently claims that she is the *cause* of the great development in educational opportunities, in freedom to work and to circulate, in the increasing willingness to face the facts of life and speak the truth. This claim she should drop. She is rather the logical result of these notions, their extreme expression. She has, however, enormous influence in keeping them alive in the great slow-moving mass of women, where the fate of new ideas rests and where they are always tried out with extreme caution. . . . She was always a tragic figure, this woman in the front of the woman's movement—driven by a great unrest, sacrificing old ideals to attain new, losing herself in a frantic and frequently blind struggle, often putting back her cause by the sad illustration she was of the price that must be paid to attain a result."

On being a journalist:

"My point of attack has always been that of a journalist after the fact. If I was tempted from the strait and narrow path of the one who seeks for that which is so and why it is so, I sooner or later returned."

On the value of one's contributions:

"I have never had illusions about the value of my individual contribution! I realized early that what a man or woman does is built on what those who have gone before have done, that its real value depends on making the matter in hand a little clearer, a little sounder for those who come after. . . ."

On standardization:

"Our people . . . live and think according to what they conceive to be national standards. They adopt them whether they suit their locality or not, and often in adopting them destroy something with individuality and charm. For the traveler it begins with the hotel, spick and span, and as like as two peas to the one in A-ville, B-ville, and so on. Over the way is a sturdy stone building dating from the days of the coach-and-four. You may sigh for its great rooms and for a sight of the old lithographs sure to be on the wall, but you know it is run down. The town could support two, and it prefers the smart and comfortable commonplace to modernizing its fine old inn.

"Look out your hotel window and you will see a smart little dress shop, a duplicate of one you have been seeing everywhere you have halted, a duplicate of many a one you have seen on New York avenues. Next door is a standardized beauty parlor, and the pretty girl who waits on you at the table has the latest coiffure and blood-red nails. She is struggling to look as she supposes girls do in Chicago or New York.

"Perhaps our national ambition to standardize ourselves has behind it the notion that democracy means standardization. But standardization is the surest way to destroy the initiative, to benumb the creative impulse above all else essential to the vitality and growth of democratic ideals."

On peace:

"If we want peace we must make men of common sense, knowing what can be done and what cannot be done, also men of goodwill."

On American political philosophy:

"I found a stable foundation of people who stayed home and went about their business in their own way. These were people who believed in freedom to work out their own salvation and asked the state nothing more than protection in this freedom.

"Democracy to them was not something which insured

them a stable livelihood. It was something which protected them while they earned a livelihood. If they failed, it was their failure. If the government did not protect them from transportation plunderers, manipulations of money, stock gambling in goods which they raised to feed the world, it was the government's failure. Then they had the right to change the government, hold it up to its duty. That was their political business."

On the nature of man:

"What we have yet to find out, apparently, is what we can expect of man under this or that circumstance, what words and what promises stir him, what persuades him to cooperation or revolt, why he follows a particular type of leader at a particular time. . . . Once we know better what we can get out of man under particular circumstances we can plan our action with something like the certainty with which the electrician plans his machine."

On old age (written at age 80):

"In spite of the notion early instilled into me that the place of the aged is in the corner resignedly waiting to die, that there is no place for their day's work in the scheme of things, that they no longer will have either the desire or the power to carry on, I find things to do which belong to me and no one else.

"It is an exciting discovery that this can be so. Old age need not be what the textbooks assure us it is. . . . My young friends laugh at me when I tell them that, in spite of creaky joints and a tremulous hand, there are satisfactions peculiar to the period, satisfactions different from those of youth, of middle age, even of that decade of the seventies which I supposed ended it all."

On the family:

"It is vulgar to leave your family if you should become richer. Through the efforts of the more fortunate members, the others can be built up, and that is what our social structure is based on. I don't like to have women more interested in politics than in their own families. The democratic way of life is built in the mind. The family unit is the beginning of that structure. It is in the family that one learns consideration of others, self-help, loyalty."

On friendship:

"A discovery which has given me joy, and which had something of the incredible about it, is the durability of friendship born at any period of one's life. Circumstances, time, separations, may have completely broken communication. The break may have been caused by complete divergence of opinion, as grave as the ghastly separations that war brings; but you pick up at the day when the friendship was—not broken but interrupted."

On life's choices:

"I have been finding it a surprising adventure, if frequently disillusioning and disturbing, to review my working life, to pick out what seems to be the reason for my going here and not there, for thinking this and not that."

On being secure:

"I'm inclined to think there is no such thing as security in this world, man being what he is, and society what it is. But how are we to make the best of it, and pull through? It's silly to think that society can make us all secure. Society isn't secure itself. An individual will be wiser to depend on his own efforts, I think."

Index

157